Careers in Focus

NONPROFIT ORGANIZATIONS

Ferguson
An imprint of Infobase Publishing

Careers in Focus: Nonprofit Organizations

Ferguson
An imprint of Infobase Publishing
132 West 31st Street
New York NY 10001

Library of Congress Cataloging-in-Publication Data

Careers in focus. Nonprofit organizations.
    p. cm. — (Careers in focus)
 Includes bibliographical references and index.
 ISBN-13: 978-0-8160-7289-7 (alk. paper)
 ISBN-10: 0-8160-7289-2 (alk. paper)
 1. Nonprofit organizations—Vocational guidance—Juvenile literature.
 HD2769.15.C37 2008
 331.702—dc22

                    2008004503

Ferguson books are available at special discounts when purchased in bulk quantities for businesses, associations, institutions, or sales promotions. Please call our Special Sales Department in New York at (212) 967-8800 or (800) 322-8755.

You can find Ferguson on the World Wide Web at http://www.fergpubco.com

Text design by David Strelecky
Cover design by Salvatore Luongo

Printed in the United States of America

Sheridan MSRF 10 9 8 7 6 5 4 3 2 1

This book is printed on acid-free paper.

Table of Contents

Introduction

In life, there are "jobs" and there are "careers." A job is often an occupation that you do because you have to pay the bills, support yourself while in school, or do for other reasons. A career is a calling that is a good match for your interests, goals, beliefs, and passions. A career is something that you can't wait to get back to every morning after a good night's rest. In short, a rewarding career defines you. It helps make you who you are.

If you are looking for a rewarding career, rather than a job, then the nonprofit sector could be just the right path for you. People who work in nonprofits help others and make the world a better place. Countless career options are available with nonprofit organizations. For example, substance abuse counselors help young people overcome addictions to alcohol, methamphetamines, or other drugs. Directors of volunteers at foundations solicit and supervise hundreds of volunteers who work on a range of projects—from rebuilding a hurricane-ravaged town on the Gulf Coast to assisting with a blood drive. Public interest lawyers represent individuals who are poor or disadvantaged. Others may be employed by advocacy groups lobbying for immigration rights, the protection of the environment, and many other issues. Grant administrators study thousands of requests from foundations for funding in order to choose the most deserving recipients. Interpreters work for nonprofit health clinics and in the legal system to provide translation services for people who are not fluent in English. Others employed by the Red Cross and fluent in Dari may be sent halfway across the world to help facilitate humanitarian services after a deadly earthquake in Afghanistan. Other career options include helping people improve their literacy (tutors), managing the financial assets of a foundation (investment professionals), helping people with disabilities stay actively involved in society (orientation and mobility specialists), performing research to help nonprofit organizations improve their chances of obtaining a grant (statisticians), and helping charities obtain financial contributions (fund-raisers).

What is a nonprofit? It is legally defined as any organization that has been granted tax-exempt status by the Internal Revenue Service. It is an organization that does not set a goal of generating a profit for its owners or shareholders. Some nonprofits may generate profit, but this profit is not given to individuals for financial gain, but used to support the goals of the organization.

Beyond financial considerations, a nonprofit can be defined as an organization that has a clear-cut mission to make the world a better place—from improving literacy in developing countries and advocating for immigration reform or the rights of the poor or disabled, to conducting research to eradicate disease and supporting the arts and humanities. According to the Foundation Center, the National Taxonomy of Exempt Entities classifies nonprofit organizations into 10 basic categories: arts, culture, and humanities; education; environment and animals; health; human services; international/foreign affairs; religious organizations; public/society benefit; mutual membership benefit organizations; and nonclassifiable organizations. Some nonprofit organizations fit into more than one of these categories; others might not be a perfect match for any of these categories.

The nonprofit sector plays a key role in the U.S. economy. Approximately 13 million people in the United States work for nonprofit organizations. About 1.4 million nonprofit organizations are registered with the Internal Revenue Service. Employment is expected to be good over the next decade with opportunities available for workers at all education and skill levels. While nonprofit workers typically earn lower salaries than their counterparts employed by for-profit organizations, they get the satisfaction of knowing that their work helps people live better and more productive lives.

Each article in this book discusses in detail a particular nonprofit-related occupation. The articles in *Careers in Focus: Nonprofit Organizations* appear in Ferguson's *Encyclopedia of Careers and Vocational Guidance,* but have been updated and revised with the latest information from the U.S. Department of Labor, professional organizations, and other sources. In addition, the following new articles have been written specifically for this book: Directors of Volunteers, Grant Administrators, Investment Professionals, Public Interest Lawyers, and Tutors and Trainers.

The following paragraphs detail the sections and features that appear in the book.

The **Quick Facts** section provides a brief summary of the career including recommended school subjects, personal skills, work environment, minimum educational requirements, salary ranges, certification or licensing requirements, and employment outlook. This section also provides acronyms and identification numbers for the following government classification indexes: the *Dictionary of Occupational Titles* (DOT), the *Guide for Occupational Exploration* (GOE), the National Occupational Classification (NOC) Index, and the Occupational Information Network (O*NET)-Standard Occupational Classification System (SOC) index. The DOT, GOE, and O*NET-SOC indexes have been created by the U.S. government; the NOC index is Canada's career classification system. Readers can use the identification numbers listed in the Quick Facts section to access further information about a career. Print editions of the DOT (*Dictionary of Occupational Titles*. Indianapolis, Ind.: JIST Works, 1991) and GOE (*Guide for Occupational Exploration*. Indianapolis, Ind.: JIST Works, 2001) are available at libraries. Electronic versions of the NOC (http://www23.hrdc-drhc.gc.ca) and O*NET-SOC (http://online.onetcenter.org) are available on the Internet. When no DOT, GOE, NOC, or O*NET-SOC numbers are present, this means that the U.S. Department of Labor or Human Resources Development Canada have not created a numerical designation for this career. In this instance, you will see the acronym "N/A," or not available.

The **Overview** section is a brief introductory description of the duties and responsibilities involved in this career. Oftentimes, a career may have a variety of job titles. When this is the case, alternative career titles are presented. Employment statistics are also provided, when available.

The **History** section describes the history of the particular job as it relates to the overall development of its industry or field.

The **Job** describes the primary and secondary duties of the job. **Requirements** discusses high school and postsecondary education and training requirements, any certification or licensing that is necessary, and other personal requirements for success in the job.

Exploring offers suggestions on how to gain experience in or knowledge of the particular job before making a firm educational and financial commitment. The focus is on what can be done while still in high school (or in the early years of college) to gain a better understanding of the job.

The **Employers** section gives an overview of typical places of employment for the job. **Starting Out** discusses the best ways to land that first job, be it through the college career services office, newspaper ads, Internet employment sites, or personal contact. The **Advancement** section describes what kind of career path to expect from the job and how to get there. **Earnings** lists salary ranges and describes the typical fringe benefits. The **Work Environment** section describes the typical surroundings and conditions of employment—whether indoors or outdoors, noisy or quiet, social or independent. Also discussed are typical hours worked, any seasonal fluctuations, and the stresses and strains of the job.

The **Outlook** section summarizes the job in terms of the general economy and industry projections. For the most part, Outlook information is obtained from the U.S. Bureau of Labor Statistics and is supplemented by information gathered from professional associations. Job growth terms follow those used in the *Occupational Outlook Handbook*. Growth described as "much faster than the average" means an increase of 27 percent or more. Growth described as "faster than the average" means an increase of 18 to 26 percent. Growth described as "about as fast as the average" means an increase of 9 to 17 percent. Growth described as "more slowly than the average" means an increase of 0 to 8 percent. "Decline" means a decrease by any amount.

Each article ends with **For More Information,** which lists organizations that provide information on training, education, internships, scholarships, and job placement.

Careers in Focus: Nonprofit Organizations also includes photographs, informative sidebars, and interviews with professionals in the field.

Alcohol and Drug Abuse Counselors

OVERVIEW

Alcohol and drug abuse counselors (sometimes called *substance abuse counselors*) work with people who abuse or are addicted to drugs or alcohol. Through individual and group counseling sessions, they help their clients understand and change their destructive substance abuse behaviors. There are about 76,000 substance-abuse counselors in the United States.

HISTORY

Throughout history people have used drugs for a variety of purposes—for healing, for religious ceremonies, to alter consciousness for self-understanding, to loosen inhibitions and have fun, or to dull the senses against emotional or physical pain. Alcohol and other substances were used in ancient Egypt, Greece, and India as offerings to spiritual beings, as well as to reach a higher consciousness. Many religions today, from Tibetan Buddhism and traditional Native American religions to Roman Catholicism, use alcohol and other consciousness-altering substances in traditional ceremonies.

Throughout the ages people have abused drugs and alcohol, too. No matter what the purpose for the initial drug use, it becomes for some people an obsession, and then an addiction. The history of treatment for substance abuse is much shorter. In the 1800s, alcoholics and morphine addicts were placed in asylums. Treatments sometimes included miracle medicines that were supposed to be quick "cures" for addicts. In the early 1900s doctors used electroshock therapies and psychosurgery to treat alcoholics.

In 1935, the Alcoholics Anonymous (AA) program was started by two men known as Bill and Dr. Bob. They helped each other achieve sobriety and continued to help others. This system of alcoholics helping other alcoholics grew into the AA movement, which is still strong today. AA's 12-step program has been adapted and used effectively to treat addictions of all kinds.

Today alcohol and a huge variety of dangerous drugs are readily available—marijuana, cocaine, LSD, heroin, inhalants, amphetamines, barbiturates, and more. Fortunately, treatment programs are also readily available for those who want them. Outpatient methadone programs give heroin addicts the medication methadone to reduce cravings for heroin and block its effects. Patients are also counseled, given vocational guidance and training, and taught how to find support services. Long-term residential programs last for several months to a year. Patients live in a drug-free environment with fellow recovering addicts and counselors. Outpatient drug-free programs use such therapies as problem-solving groups, insight-oriented psychotherapy, cognitive-behavioral therapy, and 12-step programs. Short-term inpatient programs focus on stabilizing the patient, abstinence, and lifestyle changes.

THE JOB

The main goal of alcohol and drug abuse counselors is to help patients stop their destructive behaviors. Counselors may also work with the families of clients to give them support and guidance in dealing with the problem.

Counselors begin by trying to learn about a patient's general background and history of drug or alcohol use. They may review patient records, including police reports, employment records, medical records, or reports from other counselors.

Counselors also interview the patient to determine the nature and extent of substance abuse. During an interview, the counselor asks questions about what types of substances the patient uses, how often, and for how long. The counselor may also ask patients about previous attempts to stop using the substance and about how the problem has affected their lives in various respects.

Using the information they obtain from the patient and their knowledge of substance abuse patterns, counselors formulate a program for treatment and rehabilitation. A substantial part of the rehabilitation process involves individual, group, or family counseling sessions. During individual sessions, counselors do a great deal of listening, perhaps asking appropriate questions to guide patients to insights about themselves. In group therapy sessions, counselors supervise groups of several patients, helping move their discussion in positive ways. In counseling sessions, counselors also teach patients methods of overcoming their dependencies. For example, they might help a patient develop a series of goals for behavioral change.

Counselors monitor and assess the progress of their patients. In most cases, counselors deal with several different patients in various stages of recovery—some may need help breaking the pattern of substance abuse; some may already have stopped using, but still need support; others may be recovered users who have suffered a relapse. Counselors maintain ongoing relationships with patients to help them adapt to the different recovery stages.

Working with families is another aspect of many alcohol and drug abuse counselors' jobs. They may ask a patient's family for insight into the patient's behavior. They may also teach the patient's family members how to deal with and support the patient through the recovery process.

Counselors may work with other health professionals and social agencies, including physicians, psychiatrists, psychologists, employment services, and court systems. In some cases, the counselor, with the patient's permission, may serve as a spokesperson for the patient, working with corrections officers, social workers, or employers. In other cases, a patient's needs might exceed the counselor's abilities; when this is the case, the counselor refers the patient to an appropriate medical expert, agency, or social program.

There is a substantial amount of paperwork involved in counseling alcohol and drug abusers. Detailed records must be kept on patients in order to follow their progress. For example, a report must be written after each counseling session. Counselors who work in residential treatment settings are required to participate in regular staff meetings to develop treatment plans and review patient progress. They may also meet periodically with family members or social service agency representatives to discuss patient progress and needs.

In some cases, alcohol and drug abuse counselors specialize in working with certain groups of people. Some work only with children or teenagers; others work with businesses to counsel employees who may have problems related to drugs and alcohol. In still other cases, counselors specialize in treating people who are addicted to specific drugs, such as cocaine, heroin, or alcohol. Counselors may need special training in order to work with specific groups.

REQUIREMENTS

High School

High school students who are considering a career in alcohol and drug abuse counseling should choose a curriculum that meets the requirements of the college or university they hope to attend. Typically, four years of English, history, mathematics, a foreign language, and social sciences are necessary. In addition, psychology, sociology, physiology, biology, and anatomy provide a good academic background for potential counselors.

The educational requirements for alcohol and drug abuse counselors vary greatly by state and employer. A high school education may be the minimum requirement for employers who provide on-the-job training, which ranges from six weeks to two years. These jobs, however, are becoming increasingly rare as more states are leaning toward stricter requirements for counselors.

Postsecondary Training

Some employers require an associate's degree in alcohol and drug technology. Most substance abuse counselors, however, have a bachelor's degree in counseling, psychology, health sociology, or social work. Many two- and four-year colleges now offer specific courses for students training to be substance abuse counselors.

Many counselors have a master's degree in counseling with a specialization in substance abuse counseling. Accredited graduate programs in substance abuse counseling are composed of a supervised internship as well as regular class work.

Certification or Licensing

Certification in this field, which is mandatory in some states, is available through state accreditation boards. Currently, 48 states and the District of Columbia have credentialing laws for alcohol and drug abuse counselors. These laws typically require that counselors have a minimum of a master's degree and two to three years of postacademic supervised counseling experience. Candidates must also have passed a written test.

Additionally, the NAADAC, the Association for Addiction Professionals, offers several professional designations including national certified addiction counselor, master addiction counselor, tobacco addiction specialist credential, certificate in spiritual caregiving to help addicted persons and families, and adolescent specialist endorsement.

The National Board for Certified Counselors also offers a master addiction counselor designation for counselors who hold the national certified counselor designation and meet educational and professional experience requirements.

Other Requirements

In order to be successful in this job, you should enjoy working with people. You must have compassion, good communication and listening skills, and a desire to help others. You should also be emotionally stable and able to deal with the frustrations and failures that are often a part of the job.

EXPLORING

Students interested in this career can find a great deal of information on substance abuse and substance abuse counseling at any local library. In addition, by contacting a local hospital, mental health clinic, or treatment center, it might be possible to talk with a counselor about the details of his or her job.

Volunteer work or a part-time job at a residential facility such as a hospital or treatment center is another good way of gaining experience and exploring an aptitude for counseling work. Finally, the professional and government organizations listed at the end of this article can provide information on alcohol and drug abuse counseling.

EMPLOYERS

Approximately 76,000 substance abuse counselors are employed in the United States. Counselors are hired by hospitals, private and public treatment centers, government agencies, prisons, public school systems, colleges and universities, health maintenance organizations (HMOs), crisis centers, and mental health centers. More and more frequently, large companies are hiring alcohol and drug abuse counselors as well, to deal with employee substance abuse problems.

STARTING OUT

Counselors who have completed a two- or four-year college degree might start a job search by checking with the career services office of their college or university. Those who plan to look for a position without first attending college might want to start by getting an entry-level or volunteer position in a treatment center or related agency. In this way, they can obtain practical experience and also make connections that might lead to full-time employment as a counselor.

Job seekers should also watch the classified advertisements in local newspapers. Job openings for counselors are often listed under "Alcohol and Drug Counselor," "Substance Abuse Counselor," or "Mental Health Counselor." Finally, one might consider applying directly to the personnel department of various facilities and agencies that treat alcohol and drug abusers.

ADVANCEMENT

Counselors in this field often advance initially by taking on more responsibilities and earning a higher wage. They may also better themselves by taking a similar position in a more prestigious facility, such as an upscale private treatment center.

As they obtain more experience and perhaps more education, counselors sometimes move into supervisory or administrative positions. They might become directors of substance abuse programs in mental health facilities or executive directors of agencies or clinics.

Career options are more diverse for those counselors who continue their education. They may move into research, consulting, or teaching at the college level.

EARNINGS

Salaries of alcohol and drug abuse counselors depend on education level, amount of experience, and place of employment. Generally, the more education and experience a counselor has, the higher his or her earnings will be. Counselors who work in private treatment centers also tend to earn more than their public sector counterparts.

Alcohol and drug abuse counselors earned a median annual salary of $34,040 in 2006, according to the U.S. Department of Labor. The lowest paid 10 percent earned less than $22,600. The highest paid 10 percent earned $52,340 or more. Directors of treatment programs or centers could earn considerably more that the national median salary. Almost all treatment centers provide employee benefits to their full-time counselors. Benefits usually include paid vacations and sick days, insurance, and pension plans.

WORK ENVIRONMENT

The hours that an alcohol and drug abuse counselor works depends upon where he or she is employed. Many residential treatment facilities and mental health centers—and all crisis centers—have counselors on duty during evening and weekend hours. Other employers, such as government agencies and universities, are likely to have more conventional working hours.

Work settings for counselors also vary by employer. Counselors may work in private offices, in the rooms or homes of patients, in classrooms, or in meeting rooms. In some cases, they conduct support group sessions in churches, community centers, or schools. For the most part, however, counselors work at the same work site or sites on a daily basis.

The bulk of a counselor's day is spent dealing with various people—patients, families, social workers, and health care professionals. There may be very little time during a workday for quiet reflection or organization.

Working with alcohol and drug abusers can be an emotionally draining experience. Overcoming addiction is a very hard battle, and patients respond to it in various ways. They may be resentful, angry, discouraged, or profoundly depressed. They may talk candidly with their counselors about tragic and upsetting events in their lives. Counselors spend much of their time listening to and dealing with very strong, usually negative, emotions.

This work can also be discouraging, due to a high failure rate. Many alcoholics and drug addicts do not respond to treatment and return immediately to their addictions. Even after months and sometimes years of recovery, many substance abusers suffer relapses. The counselor must learn to cope with the frustration of having his or her patients fail, perhaps repeatedly.

There is a very positive side to drug and alcohol abuse counseling, however. When it is successful, counselors have the satisfaction of knowing that they had a positive effect on someone's life. They have the reward of seeing some patients return to happy family lives and productive careers.

OUTLOOK

Employment of alcohol and drug abuse counselors is projected to grow faster than the average for all occupations through 2014, according to the U.S. Department of Labor. There are nearly 18 million alcoholics in the United States and an equal, if not greater, number of drug abusers. Because no successful method to significantly reduce drug and alcohol abuse has emerged, these numbers are not likely to decrease. Overall population growth will also lead to a need for more substance abuse counselors. Finally, many states are shifting away from criminalizing drug use, seeing it as a mental-health problem that should be treated through the medical system, not the criminal justice system.

Another reason for the expected growth in counselors' jobs is that an increasing number of employers are offering employee assistance programs that provide counseling services for mental health and alcohol and drug abuse.

Finally, many job openings will arise as a result of job turnover. Because of the stress levels and the emotional demands involved in this career, there is a high burnout rate. As alcohol and drug abuse counselors leave the field, new counselors are needed to replace them.

FOR MORE INFORMATION

For more information on substance abuse and counseling careers, contact

American Counseling Association
5999 Stevenson Avenue
Alexandria, VA 22304-3300
Tel: 800-347-6647
http://www.counseling.org

For information on certification, contact
National Board for Certified Counselors
Three Terrace Way
Greensboro, NC 27403-3660
Tel: 336-547-0607
Email: nbcc@nbcc.org
http://www.nbcc.org

For more information on alcohol and substance abuse, contact the following organizations:
National Institute on Alcohol Abuse and Alcoholism
National Institutes of Health
5635 Fishers Lane, MSC 9304
Bethesda, MD 20892-9304
Tel: 301-443-3860
http://www.niaaa.nih.gov

National Institute on Drug Abuse
National Institutes of Health
6001 Executive Boulevard, Room 5213
Bethesda, MD 20892-9561
Tel: 301-443-1124
Email: information@nida.nih.gov
http://www.nida.nih.gov

For information on certification, contact
NAADAC, The Association for Addiction Professionals
1001 North Fairfax Street, Suite 201
Alexandria, VA 22314-1797
Tel: 800-548-0497
Email: naadac@naadac.org
http://www.naadac.org

For additional information, check out the following Web site run by the Substance Abuse and Mental Health Services Administration and the U.S. Department of Health and Human Services:
National Clearinghouse for Alcohol and Drug Information
http://ncadi.samhsa.gov

Career and Employment Counselors and Technicians

OVERVIEW

Career and employment counselors, who are also known as *vocational counselors,* provide advice to individuals or groups about occupations, careers, career decision making, career planning, and other career development-related questions or conflicts. *Career guidance technicians* collect pertinent information to support both the counselor and applicant during the job search.

HISTORY

The first funded employment office in the United States was established in San Francisco in 1886. However, it was not until the turn of the century that public interest in improving educational conditions began to develop. The Civic Service House in Boston began the United States' first program of vocational guidance, and the Vocational Bureau was established in 1908 to help young people choose, train for, and enter appropriate careers.

The idea of vocational counseling became so appealing that by 1910 a national conference on vocational guidance was held in Boston. The federal government gave support to vocational counseling by initiating a program to assist veterans of World War I in read-

14

justing to civilian life. Agencies such as the Civilian Conservation Corps and the National Youth Administration made attempts at vocational counseling during the Depression years.

On June 6, 1933, the Wagner-Peyser Act established the United States Employment Service. States came into the service one by one, with each state developing its own plan under the prescribed limits of the act. By the end of World War II, the Veterans Administra-

QUICK FACTS

(continued)

GOE
12.03.01NOC
4143, 4213 (counselors)
N/A (technicians)

O*NET-SOC
13-1071.00, 13-1071.01,
    21-1012.00 (counselors)
N/A (technicians)

tion was counseling more than 50,000 veterans each month. Other state and federal government agencies now involved with vocational guidance services include the Bureau of Indian Affairs, the Bureau of Apprenticeship and Training, and the Department of Education. In 1980, the National Career Development Association (NCDA), founded in 1913, established a committee for the pre-service and in-service training of vocational guidance personnel. The NCDA established a national credentialing process in 1984.

The profession of employment counseling has become important to the welfare of society as well as to the individuals within it. Each year millions of people need help in acquiring the kinds of information that make it possible for them to take advantage of today's career opportunities.

THE JOB

Certified career counselors help people make decisions and plan life and career directions. They tailor strategies and techniques to the specific needs of the person seeking help. Counselors conduct individual and group counseling sessions to help identify life and career goals. They administer and interpret tests and inventories to assess abilities and interests and identify career options. They may use career planning and occupational information to help individuals better understand the work world. They assist in developing individualized career plans, teach job-hunting strategies and skills, and help develop resumes. Sometimes this involves resolving personal conflicts on the job. They also provide support for people experiencing job stress, job loss, and career transition.

Vocational-rehabilitation counselors work with disabled individuals to help the counselees understand what skills they have to offer to an employer. A good counselor knows the working world and how to obtain detailed information about specific jobs. To assist with career decisions, counselors must know about the availability of jobs, the probable future of certain jobs, the education or training necessary to enter them, the kinds of salary or other benefits that certain jobs offer, the conditions that certain jobs impose on employees (night work, travel, work outdoors), and the satisfaction that certain jobs provide their employees. Professional career counselors work in both private and public settings and are certified by the National Board for Certified Counselors (NBCC).

College career planning counselors and *college placement counselors* work exclusively with the students of their universities or colleges. They may specialize in some specific area appropriate to the students and graduates of the school, such as law and education, as well as in part-time and summer work, internships, and field placements. In a liberal arts college, the students may need more assistance in identifying an appropriate career. To do this, the counselor administers interest and aptitude tests and interviews students to determine their career goals.

The counselor may work with currently enrolled students who are seeking internships and other work programs while still at school. Alumni who wish to make a career change also seek the services of the career counseling and placement office at their former schools.

College placement counselors also gather complete job information from prospective employers and make the information available to interested students and alumni. Just as counselors try to find applicants for particular job listings, they also must seek out jobs for specific applicants. To do this, they will call potential employers to encourage them to consider a qualified individual.

College and career planning and placement counselors are responsible for the arrangements and details of on-campus interviews by large corporations. They also maintain an up-to-date library of vocational guidance materials and recruitment literature.

Counselors also give assistance in preparing the actual job search by helping the applicant to write resumes and letters of application, as well as by practicing interview skills through role-playing and other techniques. They also provide information on business procedures and personnel requirements in the applicant's chosen field. University-based counselors will set up online accounts on career Web sites for students, giving them access to information regarding potential employers.

Some career planning and placement counselors work with secondary school authorities, advising them on the needs of local industries and specific preparation requirements for both employment and further education. In two-year colleges the counselor may participate in the planning of course content, and in some smaller schools the counselor may be required to teach as well.

The principal duty of *career guidance technicians* is to help order, catalog, and file materials relating to job opportunities, careers, technical schools, scholarships, careers in the armed forces, and other programs. Guidance technicians also help students and teachers find materials relating to a student's interests and aptitudes. These various materials may be in the form of books, pamphlets, magazine articles, microfiche, videos, computer software, or other media.

Often, career guidance technicians help students take and score self-administered tests that determine their aptitude and interest in different careers or job-related activities. If the career guidance center has audiovisual equipment, such as VCRs, DVD players, or film or slide projectors, career guidance technicians are usually responsible for the equipment.

REQUIREMENTS

High School

In order to work in the career and employment counseling field, you must have at least a high school diploma. For most jobs in the field, however, higher education is required. In high school, in addition to studying a core curriculum, with courses in English, history, mathematics, and biology, you should take courses in psychology and sociology. You will also find it helpful to take business and computer science classes.

Postsecondary Training

In some states, the minimum educational requirement in career and vocational counseling is a graduate degree in counseling or a related field from a regionally accredited higher education institution, and a completed supervised counseling experience, which includes career counseling. A growing number of institutions offer post-master's degrees with training in career development and career counseling. Such programs are highly recommended if you wish to specialize in vocational and career counseling. These programs are frequently called advanced graduate specialist programs or certificates of advanced study programs.

For a career as a college career planning and placement counselor, the minimum educational requirement is commonly a master's degree in guidance and counseling, education, college student personnel work, behavioral science, or a related field. Graduate work includes courses in vocational and aptitude testing, counseling techniques, personnel management and occupational research, industrial relations, and group dynamics and organizational behavior.

As in any profession, there is usually an initial period of training for newly hired counselors and counselor trainees. Some of the skills you will need as an employment counselor, such as testing-procedures skills and interviewing skills, can be acquired only through on-the-job training.

When hiring a career guidance technician, most employers look for applicants who have completed two years of training beyond high school, usually at a junior, community, or technical college. These two-year programs, which usually lead to an associate's degree, may combine classroom instruction with practical or sometimes even on-the-job experience.

Certification or Licensing
The NBCC offers the national certified counselor (NCC) designation as well as the national certified school counselor (NCSC) designation. In order to apply for the NCC, you must have earned a master's degree with a major study in counseling and you must pass the National Counselor Examination. NCCs are certified for a period of five years. In order to be recertified, you must complete 100 contact clock hours of continuing education or pass the examination again. In order to receive the NCSC credential, you must complete the above requirements, plus gain field experience in school counseling as a graduate student and then complete three years of postgraduate supervised school counseling. Many states require some type of credentialing or certification for counselors, and all states require those who work in school settings to be certified.

Other Requirements
In order to succeed as a career counselor, you must have a good background in education, training, employment trends, the current labor market, and career resources. You should be able to provide your clients with information about job tasks, functions, salaries, requirements, and the future outlook of broad occupational fields.

Knowledge of testing techniques and measures of aptitude, achievement, interests, values, and personality is required. The ability to evaluate job performance and individual effectiveness is helpful. You must also have management and administrative skills.

EXPLORING
Summer work in an employment agency is a good way to explore the field of employment counseling. Interviewing the director of a

A career counselor assists a job hunter. *(Bob Daemmrich, The Image Works)*

public or private agency might give you a better understanding of what the work involves and the qualifications such an organization requires of its counselors.

If you enjoy working with others, you will find helpful experiences working in the dean's or counselor's office. Many schools offer opportunities in peer tutoring, both in academics and in career guidance-related duties. (If your school does not have such a program in place, consider putting together a proposal to institute one. Your guidance counselor should be able to help you with this.) Your own experience in seeking summer and part-time work is also valuable in learning what job seekers must confront in business or industry. You could write a feature story for your school newspaper on your and others' experiences in the working world.

If you are interested in becoming a career counselor, you should seek out professional career counselors and discuss the field with them. Most people are happy to talk about what they do.

While in high school, consider working part time or as a volunteer in a library. Such work can provide you with some of the basic skills for learning about information resources, cataloging, and filing. In addition, assisting schools or clubs with any media presentations, such as video or slide shows, will help you become familiar with the equipment used by counselors. You may also find it helpful to read publications relating to this field, such as *The National Certified Counselor* news-letter (http://www.nbcc.org/users/productseekers.htm).

EMPLOYERS

There are approximately 248,000 educational, vocational, and school counselors employed in the United States. Career and employment counselors work in guidance offices of high schools, colleges, and universities. They are also employed by state, federal, and other bureaus of employment, and by social service agencies.

STARTING OUT

Journals specializing in information for career counselors frequently have job listings or information on job hotlines and services. School career services offices also are a good source of information, both because of their standard practice of listing job openings from participating firms and because schools are a likely source of jobs for you as a career counselor. Placement officers will be aware of which schools are looking for applicants.

To enter the field of college career planning and placement, you might consider working for your alma mater as an assistant in the college or university career services office. Other occupational areas that provide an excellent background for college placement work include teaching, business, public relations, previous placement training, positions in employment agencies, and experience in psychological counseling.

Career guidance technicians should receive some form of career placement from schools offering training in that area. Newspapers may list entry-level jobs. One of the best methods, however, is to contact libraries and education centers directly to inquire about their needs for assistance in developing or staffing their career guidance centers.

ADVANCEMENT

Employment counselors in federal or state employment services or in other vocational counseling agencies are usually considered trainees for the first six months of their employment. During this time, they learn the specific skills that will be expected of them during their careers with these agencies. The first year of a new counselor's employment is probationary.

Positions of further responsibility include supervisory or administrative work, which may be attained by counselors after several years of experience on the job. Advancement to administrative positions often means giving up the actual counseling work, which is not an advantage to those who enjoy working with people in need of counseling.

Opportunity for advancement for college counselors—to assistant and associate placement director, director of student personnel services, or similar administrative positions—depends largely on the type of college or university and the size of the staff. In general, a doctorate is preferred and may be necessary for advancement.

With additional education, career guidance technicians can advance to become career and employment counselors.

EARNINGS

Salaries vary greatly within the career and vocational counseling field. The U.S. Department of Labor (DOL) places career counselors within the category of educational, vocational, and school counselors. The median yearly earnings for this group were $47,530 in 2006, according to the DOL. The lowest paid 10 percent of these workers earned $27,240 per year, and the highest paid 10 percent made $75,920 annually. The department further broke down salaries by type of employer: those working for elementary and secondary schools had mean annual incomes of $55,560 in 2006; for junior colleges, $53,650; for colleges and universities, $44,730; for individual and family services, $35,020; and for vocational rehabilitation services, $34,320. Annual earnings of career counselors vary greatly among educational institutions, with larger institutions offering the highest salaries. Counselors in business or industry tend to earn higher salaries.

In private practice, the salary range is even wider. Some practitioners earn as little as $20,000 per year, and others, such as elite "headhunters" who recruit corporate executives and other high-salaried positions, earn in excess of $100,000 per year.

Salaries for career guidance technicians vary according to education and experience and the geographic location of the job. In general, career guidance technicians who are graduates of two-year post high school training programs can expect to receive starting salaries averaging $20,000 to $25,000 a year.

Benefits depend on the employer, but they usually include paid holidays and vacation time, retirement plans, and, for those at some educational institutions, reduced tuition.

WORK ENVIRONMENT

Employment counselors usually work about 40 hours a week, but some agencies are more flexible. Counseling is done in offices designed to be free from noise and distractions, to allow confidential discussions with clients.

College career planning and placement counselors also normally work a 40-hour week, although irregular hours and overtime are frequently required during the peak recruiting period. They generally work on a 12-month basis.

Career guidance technicians work in very pleasant surroundings, usually in the career guidance office of a college or vocational school. They will interact with a great number of students, some of whom are eagerly looking for work, and others who are more tense and anxious. The technician must remain unruffled in order to ease any tension and provide a quiet atmosphere.

OUTLOOK

Opportunities in the field of employment counseling are expected to grow faster than the average for all occupations through 2014, according to the U.S. Department of Labor. One reason for this growth is increased school enrollments, even at the college level, which means more students needing the services of career counselors. Another reason is that there are more counselor jobs than graduates of counseling programs. Opportunities should also be available in government agencies as many states institute welfare-to-work programs or simply cut welfare benefits. And finally, in this age of outsourcing and lack of employment security, "downsized" workers, those re-entering the workforce, and those looking for second careers all create a need for the skills of career and employment counselors.

FOR MORE INFORMATION

For a variety of career resources for career seekers and career counseling professionals, contact the following organizations:

American Counseling Association
5999 Stevenson Avenue
Alexandria, VA 22304-3300
Tel: 800-347-6647
http://www.counseling.org

Career Planning & Adult Development Network
543 Vista Mar Avenue
Pacifica, CA 94044-1951
Tel: 650-359-6911

Email: admin@careernetwork.org
http://www.careernetwork.org

For resume and interview tips, general career information, and advice from experts, contact or visit the following Web site:
National Association of Colleges and Employers (NACE)
62 Highland Avenue
Bethlehem, PA 18017-9085
Tel: 800-544-5272
http://www.naceweb.org

For information on certification, contact
National Board for Certified Counselors
3 Terrace Way
Greensboro, NC 27403-3660
Tel: 336-547-0607
Email: nbcc@nbcc.org
http://www.nbcc.org

For more information on career counselors, contact
National Career Development Association
305 North Beech Circle
Broken Arrow, OK 74012-2293
Tel: 918-663-7060
http://ncda.org

Directors of Volunteers

QUICK FACTS

School Subjects
Business
Psychology

Personal Skills
Helping/teaching
Leadership/management

Work Environment
Primarily indoors
Primarily multiple locations

Minimum Education Level
Bachelor's degree

Salary Range
$32,646 to $33,061 to
$74,287

Certification or Licensing
Voluntary

Outlook
About as fast as the average

DOT
187

GOE
12.01.01

NOC
0314

O*NET-SOC
11-9151.00

OVERVIEW

A *director of volunteers* employed by a nonprofit organization is responsible for recruiting, training, and placing volunteers in a variety of positions. Depending on the size of the organization and the scope of its mission, the director of volunteers may oversee anywhere from a few volunteers working a few hours a week on a short-term project to thousands of volunteers committed to a longer time frame. The director of volunteers is fully involved in all aspects of recruiting and training volunteers including raising awareness of the organization's mission, planning events, and fund-raising.

HISTORY

Ever since the first nonprofit organizations were founded, volunteers have been needed to help these organizations meet their goals. The management of volunteers in small organizations was usually handled by one or more individuals in the organization in addition to their primary job duties. But in large foundations with significant budgets and many projects, managers soon realized that they needed a trained professional to recruit, train, and place volunteers to best serve the needs of the organization. This led to the creation of the career of director of volunteers.

THE JOB

Many nonprofit organizations rely on the strength of their volunteers to meet their mission goals. Some nonprofits operate with a full staff of volunteers. It can be a tremendous undertaking to organize, train, and monitor volunteers—each with his or her skill level, personality, and time commitment. Most nonprofit organizations, especially those dealing with a volunteer pool of hundreds or even thousands, rely on a director of volunteers to oversee the process.

The director of volunteers must first assess the needs of his or her organization. Habitat for Humanity International, for example, is an international nonprofit organization that aims to erase poverty housing and homelessness. A director of volunteers working for this organization would first identify the needs of a particular project—for example, rebuilding an area affected by a recent natural disaster. He or she would determine the types of volunteers needed—various construction crews, engineers, architects, as well as other related workers—and then recruit the workers to tackle the project.

Recruiting volunteers is an important task for the director. Volunteers are not paid, so they must agree to do the work based solely on their good intentions and commitment to help others. Awareness for a project needs to be raised in order to attract and motivate new volunteers. The director often works with the nonprofit's marketing or public relations department to get coverage in local papers, on broadcast stations, or though press kits or mass mailings. He or she often appeals to local businesses, schools, religious organizations, and social groups for volunteers.

Directors are responsible for creating a volunteer descriptor that explains the particular assignment and its purpose, the location of the project, and skills and abilities required. Commitment expectations also need to be clearly identified. Some nonprofit projects, such as volunteering for a local blood drive benefiting the Red Cross, may last a few hours. Other projects, such as participating in a Big Brothers Big Sisters program, may call for a year-long commitment.

Volunteers may sign up through an agency's Web site, headquarters, or local chapter, or may join a group through their school, church, or local government. Names of potential volunteers are then forwarded directly to the director.

Once a pool of volunteers is assembled, the director begins to identify and group them according to their skills and time commitment requirements. Certain skills or educational backgrounds are mandatory for certain volunteer positions. Volunteers drawing blood at a Red Cross blood drive, for example, would need to be nurses, physicians, or phlebotomy technicians.

Once candidates are identified, the director or an assistant conducts a short interview with the individual to ascertain if he or she is a good fit for the project. The director also conducts background checks at this time, depending on the size and resources of the organization and the nature of the project. Volunteers are usually asked to supply a list of character references, but may be asked to undergo a more thorough background clearance—especially when the project involves children. It is the director's responsibility to reject a potential volunteer, especially when the individual's motives for volunteering are in doubt. In such cases, being a good judge of character is imperative.

Many volunteers come as part of a group. The director works with the group to accommodate its time frame—whether it is a short amount of time, say during a lunch hour, or a larger commitment block such as during a school's spring break.

The director arranges for training and orientation for all volunteers. The amount and level of training offered will depend on the project at hand. At a vertical climb in a skyscraper to raise awareness for the American Lung Association, volunteers helped with many different aspects of the event. Volunteers in charge of positioning the athletes at the starting line or dispensing water and bananas at the finish were given training and orientation, but to a lesser degree than those volunteers assigned to administer first aid. While many of these volunteers were already in the medical field, their training and orientation included learning about exit routes from the venue as well as the proper way to document medical treatment provided to injured or ill participants.

Recognition of volunteers is important, even after the project or event is completed. Directors work to thank volunteers on large projects by holding award dinners or implementing a Volunteer of the Month award and publicizing it in local newspapers or on radio or television. Many directors may write personal thank you notes to volunteers or award them certificates of achievement.

The director of volunteers may be responsible for other duties such as fund-raising, development of educational programs, and media relations. Some directors may be in charge of contacting area business to solicit monetary donations or materials. For example, directors working for a literacy group or mentor group may appeal to local publishing companies for donations of books or magazines to help with their cause. Some directors may be responsible for summarizing project data and taking photos for use in press releases and media kits.

REQUIREMENTS

High School

In high school, take as many college preparatory classes as possible. Courses in English and speech will help you communicate effectively with volunteers and coworkers. Computer science classes—especially

Facts About Volunteering, 2006

- Approximately 61.2 million people in the United States—or 26.7 percent of the population—were active volunteers between September 2005 and September 2006.
- Volunteers spent a median of 52 hours participating in volunteer activities between September 2005 and September 2006.
- Individuals age 35 to 54 were the most likely to volunteer (31.2 percent). People in their early 20s were the least likely to volunteer (17.8 percent).
- Volunteer rates by ethnicity were: whites (28.3 percent), blacks (19.2 percent), Asians (18.5 percent), and Hispanics (13.9 percent).
- The most popular volunteer activities were fund-raising (10.9 percent) and tutoring or teaching (10.8 percent).

Sources: U.S. Department of Labor

those in database management—will help you learn how to use computers to manage information on volunteers and projects. Other useful classes include mathematics, psychology, business, and marketing.

Postsecondary Training
While most directors of volunteers hold a bachelor's degree or better, there is no preferred college major. Directors enter this field with a variety of educational backgrounds suited to the focus of their nonprofit organization. Courses in communications, business management, marketing and social work, however, have proven helpful to many directors.

Certification or Licensing
Many state-level volunteer administration associations offer voluntary certification to directors of volunteers. Performing a keyword search on the Internet using phrases such as "association for volunteer administration" or "state volunteering association" should help you locate an association in your state.

Other Requirements
A desire to help others is the most important personal trait for this career. Organization, compassion, and patience are other personal traits commonly possessed by directors of volunteers. They must be

positive motivators and teachers in order to train workers who are earning nothing more than the satisfaction of helping others and making a difference in the world.

EXPLORING

Do you aspire to become a director of volunteers? If so, volunteering at your favorite organization or charity is a great start. You could dispense water to runners at a local marathon, keep track of donations at a women's shelter, or record print material for the blind. Conducting an information interview with a director of volunteers at a local nonprofit organization will also give you a great introduction to the field. Finally, reading professional journals, such as the *International Journal of Volunteer Administration* (http://www.ijova.org), will introduce you to important issues in the field.

EMPLOYERS

Employment prospects for executive positions are best in major cities—such as New York, Chicago, and Washington, D.C.—where the headquarters of many of the larger nonprofits are located. However, many nonprofits are international, and therefore have offices located worldwide. For example Amnesty International, an organization that is committed to preserving human rights, manages volunteers in 88 local offices throughout the Americas, Europe, Asia, and Africa.

In addition, thousands of smaller, local nonprofit groups are located throughout the United States. Each relies on the work of its volunteer workforce and turns to volunteer organizers and directors for management.

STARTING OUT

Many salaried workers in nonprofit organizations start out as volunteers. After some experience as a volunteer with a particular group, you may be asked to become a team leader, project head, or assistant coordinator who is responsible for a small group of volunteers.

Many schools expect students to earn a certain amount of service hours—time spent volunteering at various jobs, organizations, or causes. Service hours are required in order to graduate, but they also serve as a valuable stepping-stone for a career in nonprofit volunteering. Check with your guidance counselor for programs affiliated with your school, the position's duties and responsibilities, and time commitment.

Volunteers in the Summer in the City program in Detroit, Michigan, build a small park in the inner city. The program brings young people from Detroit and the suburbs together to participate in community improvement projects. *(Jim West, The Image Works)*

ADVANCEMENT

With ample experience, a director of volunteers may advance to become an *executive director of volunteers*. These professionals manage the volunteer activities of multiple chapters of an organization. Others advance to become executive directors of their organizations, association executives, or make a lateral move to a similar position at a larger, more prestigious organization.

EARNINGS

According to *Compensation in Nonprofit Organizations 2006*, a report from Abbott, Langer & Associates, directors of volunteers had median annual incomes of $33,061 in 2006. A 2005/2006 *Nonprofit Times* survey reported that salaries for directors of volunteers ranged from $32,646 for those employed by organizations with budgets of $500,000 to $999,000 to $74,287 for directors employed by organizations with budgets of $50 million or more. Most directors of volunteers receive benefits such as health insurance, sick leave, paid holidays, retirement plans, and savings plans.

WORK ENVIRONMENT

The work environment for directors of volunteers varies depending on several factors such as the size of the organization, its funding, and the scope and nature of its mission.

Directors of volunteers employed at organizations such as Reading for the Blind & Dyslexic work indoors. They audition, train, and schedule volunteers within the comfort of indoor recording studios.

Other organizations may require directors of volunteers to work both indoors and outdoors depending on the task at hand. Volunteer managers for the Desert Botanical Garden in Arizona, for example, may find themselves working inside comfortable offices one day, and outdoors in hot, dry weather the next. Indoor tasks may include screening and orienting volunteers, producing promotional materials to recruit new volunteers, event planning, and scheduling. Outdoor tasks may include working in the gardens alongside volunteer gardeners and landscapers, or managing volunteer shifts at a plant sale or seasonal festival.

Some travel to schools and libraries and may be required to promote the organization's products and services and to recruit new volunteers.

OUTLOOK

Employment for directors of volunteers is expected to grow about as fast as the average in the next decade. Despite the fact that studies have shown that organizations with professional directors of volunteers raise more money and have a stronger volunteer base, the position is often the first to be cut when an organization's budget is tight. Directors of volunteers with advanced training and experience will have the best employment prospects.

FOR MORE INFORMATION

For information on nonprofit organizations, contact the following organizations:

Council on Foundations
1828 L Street, NW, Suite 300
Washington, DC 20036-5104
Tel: 202-466-6512
Email: info@cof.org
http://www.cof.org

Foundation Center
79 Fifth Avenue & 16th Street
New York, NY 10003-3076
Tel: 800-424-9836
http://foundationcenter.org

National Council of Nonprofit Associations
1101 Vermont Avenue, NW, Suite 1002
Washington, DC 20005-3560
Tel: 202-962-0322
http://www.ncna.org

Fund-Raisers

QUICK FACTS

School Subjects
Business
English
Mathematics

Personal Skills
Communication/ideas
Leadership/management

Work Environment
Primarily indoors
Primarily one location

Minimum Education Level
Bachelor's degree

Salary Range
$20,000 to $71,305 to
$200,000+

Certification or Licensing
Recommended

Outlook
About as fast as the average

DOT
293

GOE
N/A

NOC
N/A

O*NET-SOC
N/A

OVERVIEW

Fund-raisers develop and coordinate the plans by which charity organizations gain financial contributions, generate publicity, and fulfill fiscal objectives. Fund-raisers are employed at a variety of nonprofit organizations, including those in the arts, social service, health care, and educational fields, as well as at private consulting firms around the country.

HISTORY

Organized fund-raising, or philanthropy, is a relatively modern refinement of the old notion of charity. It may be surprising to learn that some people make a living by organizing charity appeals and fund drives, but philanthropy ranks among the 10 largest industries in the United States. The most familiar forms of fund-raising are the much publicized and visible types, such as telethons, direct-mail campaigns, and canned food drives. Successful fund-raising does not depend on a high profile; however, it often requires marketing the appeal for funds to the people most likely to donate. Successful fund-raising requires careful planning, staffing, and execution. An experienced fund-raiser can make all the difference between a successful revenue campaign and a disappointing one.

THE JOB

Fund-raising combines many different skills, such as financial management and accounting, public relations, marketing, human resources, management, and media communications. To be successful, the appeal for funds has to target the people most likely to donate, and donors have to be convinced of the good work being done by the cause they are supporting. To do this, fund-raisers need strong media support and savvy public relations. Fund-raisers also have to bring together people, including volunteers, paid staff, board members, and other community contacts, and direct them toward the common goal of enriching the charity.

To illustrate how a revenue-raising campaign might be conducted, take a look at a private high school, Branton Academy, which is trying to raise money to build a new facility. The principal of Branton approaches a fund-raising consulting firm to study the possible approaches to take. Building a new facility and acquiring the land would cost the academy approximately $800,000. The fund-raising firm's first job is to ask difficult questions about the realism of the academy's goal. What were the results of the academy's last fund-raising effort? Do the local alumni tend to respond to solicitations for revenue? Are the alumni active leaders in the community, and can their support be counted on? Are there enough potential givers besides alumni in the area to reach the goal? Are there enough volunteers on hand to launch a revenue campaign? What kind of publicity, good and bad, has the academy recently generated? What other charities, especially private schools, are trying to raise money in the area at that time?

Once the fund-raising consulting firm has a solid understanding of what the academy is trying to accomplish, it conducts a feasibility study to determine whether there is community support for such a project. If community support exists—that is, if it appears that the fund-raising drive could be a success—the consulting firm works with officials at Branton to draft a fund-raising plan. The plan will describe in detail the goals of the fund-raising appeal, the steps to be taken to meet those goals, the responsibilities of the paid staff and volunteers, budget projections for the campaign, and other important policies. For Branton Academy, the fund-raising consultant might suggest a three-tiered strategy for the campaign: a bicycle marathon by the students to generate interest and initiate the publicity campaign, followed by a month-long phone drive to people in the area, and ending with a formal dinner dance that charges $50 or more per person.

Once the plan is agreed upon, the fund-raising consultants organize training for the volunteers, especially those in phone solicitation, and give them tips on how to present the facts of the campaign to potential contributors and get them to support Branton's efforts. The fund-raisers make arrangements for publicity and press coverage, sometimes employing a professional publicist, so that people will hear about the

Philanthropic Giving

More than $295 billion was given to a wide variety of organizations in 2006. The following table offers a breakdown of contributors:

Contributor	Amount Given	Percent of Total
Individuals	$222.89 billion	75.6
Foundations	$36.50 billion	12.4
Bequests	$22.91 billion	7.8
Corporations	$12.72 billion	4.2

Source: *Giving USA 2007*

campaign before they are approached for donations. During the campaign, the consultants and the staff of Branton will research possible large contributors, such as corporations, philanthropic foundations, and wealthy individuals. These potential sources of revenue will receive special attention and personal appeals from fund-raising professionals and Branton's principal and trustees. If the fund-raising effort is a success, Branton Academy will have both the funds it needs to expand and a higher profile in the community.

This example is fairly clear and straightforward, but the financial needs of most charities are so complex that a single, month-long campaign would be only part of their fund-raising plans. The American Cancer Society, for instance, holds many charity events in an area every year, in addition to occasional phone drives, marathons, year-round magazine and television advertising, and special appeals to large individual donors. Fund-raisers who work on the staff of charities and nonprofit organizations may need to push several fund drives at the same time, balancing their efforts between long-range endowment funds and special projects. Every nonprofit organization has its own unique goals and financial needs; therefore, fund-raisers have to tailor their efforts to the characteristics of the charity or organization involved. This requires imagination, versatility, and resourcefulness on the fund-raiser's part. The proper allocation of funds is also a weighty responsibility. Fund-raisers also must have strong people skills, especially communications, because their personal contact with volunteers, donors, board members, community groups, local leaders, and members of the press may be an important factor in the success of any revenue appeal.

REQUIREMENTS

High School

To pursue a career in fund-raising, you should follow a college preparatory curriculum. English, creative writing, speech, mathematics, business, and history classes are recommended, as well as a foreign language, bookkeeping, and computer training. Extracurricular activities such as student council and community outreach programs can help you cultivate important leadership qualities and give you a taste of what fund-raising work requires.

Postsecondary Training

Only a small number of colleges offer degrees or certificates in fund-raising. However, colleges are increasingly offering courses in the broader field of philanthropy. Most fund-raisers have earned a university degree. A broad liberal arts background, with special attention to the social sciences, is a great benefit to fund-raisers because of the nature of most fund-raising work. Specialized degrees that could benefit fund-raisers include communications, psychology, sociology, public relations, business administration, education, and journalism. This type of education will give fund-raisers insight into the concerns and efforts of most nonprofit organizations and how to bring their worthwhile efforts to the public's attention. Courses in economics, accounting, and mathematics are also very useful.

Certification or Licensing

While not required, CFRE International offers a certified fund raising executive (CFRE) program. This certification process is endorsed by leading philanthropic associations, including the Association of Fundraising Professionals. Those who hold certification must become recertified every three years.

Other Requirements

Because fund-raisers need to be able to talk and work with all kinds of people, you will need to be outgoing and friendly. Leadership is also an important quality, because you need to gain the respect of volunteers and inspire them to do their best. Their enthusiasm for a campaign can be a major factor in other people's commitment to the cause.

EXPLORING

The best way to gauge your interest in a fund-raising career is to volunteer to help at churches, social agencies, health charities, schools, and other organizations for their revenue drives. All of these groups are looking for volunteers and gladly welcome any help they can get. You will be able to observe the various efforts that go into a successful fund-raising drive and the work and dedication of professional fund-raisers. In this way, you can judge whether you enjoy this type of work. Try to interview the fund-raisers that you meet for their advice in ways to gain more experience and find employment.

EMPLOYERS

Fund-raisers are usually employed in one of three different ways. They may be members of the staff of the organization or charity in question. For example, many colleges and hospitals maintain fund-raisers on staff, sometimes referred to as *solicitors,* who report to the development director or outreach coordinator. They may also be employed by fund-raising consulting firms, which for a fee will help nonprofit organizations manage their campaigns, budget their money and resources, determine the feasibility of different revenue programs, and counsel them in other ways. Many for-profit companies also have fund-raisers on staff to plan and conduct charity social events, such as fund-raising balls, formal dinners, telethons, walk-a-thons, parties, or carnivals. Corporations perform these philanthropic functions both to help the charity and the community and to generate favorable publicity for themselves.

STARTING OUT

The key to a job in fund-raising is experience. Both private consultants and nonprofit staffs prefer to hire fund-raisers who already have worked on other revenue drives. Because their budgets are always tight, nonprofit organizations are especially reluctant to hire people who need to be trained from scratch. Some small organizations that do not have a budget to hire full-time fund-raisers may use volunteers.

Colleges offer many opportunities for gaining experience, because nearly every college has at least one staff member (more than likely an entire office) in charge of generating donations from alumni and other sources. These staff members will have useful advice to give on their profession, including private consulting firms that hire fund-raisers. A student may have to serve as a volunteer for such a firm first to get to know the people involved and potentially to be considered for a permanent position.

Internet Becoming Popular— and Lucrative—Fund-Raising Tool

Electronic gifts to large U.S. charities increased from $880.7 million in 2005 to $1.2 billion in 2006 (an increase of 37 percent), according to the *Chronicle of Philanthropy*. And online fund-raising offers fund-raisers a bigger bang for their buck, at least according to a study by Kintera Inc., an online services provider. The organization gathered data on 625 fund-raising events, 430,000 participants, and 800,000 transactions and found that fund-raisers who used e-mail to solicit donations raised an average of $327 from 6.99 donors, while those not using e-mail raised an average of $55 from 1.48 donors. The study also found that the more e-mails fund-raisers sent, the more funds were raised both online and offline.

These trends suggest that there will be strong demand for fund-raisers with strong computer skills and knowledge of online fund-raising techniques.

ADVANCEMENT

In a private consulting firm, fund-raisers can advance to higher-paying jobs by gaining experience and developing skills. As responsibilities increase, fund-raisers may be put in charge of certain aspects of a campaign, such as the direct-mail or corporate appeal, or may even direct an entire campaign. Those who work for a large social service or nonprofit agency will also find that promotions are determined by skill and creativity in handling difficult assignments. After gaining experience with several nonprofit agencies, some fund-raisers move on and start counseling businesses of their own.

EARNINGS

While beginning fund-raisers do not earn much ($20,000 to $25,000), their salaries will increase as they gain experience or lead successful revenue efforts. In a 2007 survey conducted by the Association of Fundraising Professionals, members of the association reported an average salary of $71,305. Fund-raisers who held the certified fund raising executive designation earned an average $20,000 more than respodents who were not certified. The average salary of CFRE certificants was $85,032 in 2007. Experienced fund-raisers can be very highly paid, and some of the best earn more than $200,000 a year. To attract and retain experienced fund-raisers, private agencies and nonprofit organizations will also offer competitive salaries and good benefits. While some nonprofit organizations may offer performance bonuses, they are not usually tied directly to the amounts raised.

Benefits for fund-raisers often are equivalent to other professional business positions, including paid vacations, group insurance plans, and paid sick days.

WORK ENVIRONMENT

The working conditions for professional fund-raisers can sometimes be less than ideal. During revenue campaigns, they may have to work in temporary facilities. Their working hours can be irregular, because they have to meet and work with volunteers, potential donors, and other people whenever those people are available. When campaigns become intense, fund-raisers may have to work long hours, seven days a week. With all the activity that goes on during a campaign, the atmosphere may become stressful, especially as deadlines draw near. So many demands are put on fund-raisers during a campaign—to arrange work schedules, meet with community groups, track finances, and so on—that they must be very organized, flexible, and committed to the overall strategy for the appeal.

OUTLOOK

The job prospects of people who wish to become fund-raisers are good. As federal funding of nonprofit organizations continues to decrease, these groups have to raise operating revenue themselves. They are discovering that hiring full-time fund-raisers is a smart investment. Private fund-raising counseling firms have also reported a need for skilled employees. These firms usually require some experience, but since there are so many fund-raising causes that will eagerly welcome volunteers, interested people should have no problem gaining experience. Both public agencies and private consulting firms keep a full-time staff of fund-raisers, and they may hire part-time workers during special periods and campaigns.

FOR MORE INFORMATION

The following is a professional association for individuals responsible for generating philanthropic support for nonprofits. It provides educational programs, a resource center, conference, and bimonthly journal.

Association of Fundraising Professionals
4300 Wilson Boulevard, Suite 300
Arlington, VA 22203-4179
Tel: 703-684-0410
http://www.afpnet.org

For information on certification as a certified fund-raising executive, contact
CFRE International
4900 Seminary Road, Suite 670
Alexandria, VA 22311-1811
Tel: 703-820-5555
Email: info@cfre.org
http://www.cfre.org

This organization is a coalition of consulting firms working in the nonprofit sector.
Giving Institute: Leading Consultants to Non-Profits
4700 West Lake Avenue
Glenview, IL 60025-1468
Tel: 800-462-2372
Email: info@givinginstitute.org
http://www.aafrc.org

This newspaper for the nonprofit world is published every other week.
The Chronicle of Philanthropy
http://philanthropy.com

Grant Administrators

QUICK FACTS

School Subjects
Business
Mathematics

Personal Skills
Helping/teaching
Leadership/management

Work Environment
Primarily indoors
One location with some
  travel

Minimum Education Level
Some postsecondary training

Salary Range
$41,569 to $55,000 to
  $84,654+

Certification or Licensing
None available

Outlook
About as fast as the average

DOT
N/A

GOE
N/A

NOC
N/A

O*NET-SOC
21-1099.99

OVERVIEW

Grant administrators are employed by foundations to evaluate nonprofit organizations and charities as candidates for possible financial assistance. At large foundations, grant administrators may review and work with a grant application at all levels of the process before it is brought to the attention of the grant committee or board members. At smaller foundations, the grant administrator may have a more active role in the approval or rejection of an application.

HISTORY

In the early days of foundations and other philanthropic organizations, executive directors or their support staff typically sifted through the thousands of requests received for financial assistance. They decided which applicants deserved funds and which did not. After choosing the organizations or individuals that would be awarded funds, they also had to manage the grant process—from the initial awarding of funds to the closing of the grant after the project was completed.

As foundations grew in size and the amount of money they were able to award to worthy organizations increased, so did the workload for directors and support staff. It soon became apparent that a specially trained worker was needed to manage the grant process from start to finish. This professional became known as the grant administrator or grant manager. Nearly every major foundation or philanthropic organization today has a grant administrator who is responsible for managing the grant-making process.

THE JOB

Foundations, whether funded privately or through the community, are charitable organizations that provide funding or other support to organizations that meet their expectations. For example, the Bill and Melinda Gates Foundation, one of the largest in the world, has specific models of projects it chooses to fund. In the United States, the foundation favors programs that reduce inequities in the field of early education, increase the high school graduation rate, and award college scholarships to low-income, minority students. It is the role of the grant administrator to serve as a liaison between the foundation and deserving organizations or individuals.

The grant process begins when an organization submits an application to the foundation for funding. Before pursuing a formal application, some foundations advise organizations to first send a letter of inquiry to determine if its project meets the foundation's current interests. Most foundations have a print or online application that identifies the type of organization requesting assistance, the scope of the project, and other important details such as population and location served and the size of the award. Other foundations prefer a written proposal as opposed to a standard application.

Once the application or proposal is received by the foundation, the grant administrator creates a file and codes the application or proposal according to a particular classification—subject, type of recipient organization, population groups, type of award, geographic focus, etc. Grant administrators then review the application or proposal. Any problems, such as missing or incomplete information, are addressed and corrected. It is important for the grant administrator to determine if the scope of the proposal is within the criteria of the foundation, as all grants are listed and described on the foundation's Web site and in annual reports. Grant administrators must also ensure that the proposed project complies with regulations established by the Internal Revenue Service, as well as other governmental guidelines. The grant administrator, together with foundation board members, its trustees, and program officers, decide which projects will be awarded grants. Foundations have a set annual budget from which to appropriate funds. For example, the Ford Foundation, one of the largest in the United States, makes tentative plans for about 65 percent of its giving budget, the rest is allocated for unexpected, or new proposals.

The number of applications received annually varies depending on the size of the foundation and its available funding. The Ford Foundation receives about 40,000 grant requests a year, of which 2,500 are approved, with some grants exceeding millions of dollars. Foundations with smaller holdings receive considerably fewer applications.

Once the application or proposal is approved, grant administrators create an award agreement to be signed by the foundation trustees and the grantees, or recipients, of the award. This award agreement details the scope and time frame of the project, as well as a payout schedule for grant funding.

Monitoring the project is also the responsibility of the grant administrator. He or she will receive updates and reports from the grantee on a monthly or yearly basis, depending on the project. The grant administrator makes sure that the grantee meets the approved objectives and keeps within the interests of the foundation. At times, the grant administrator may request a meeting with the grantee or schedule an onsite visit to ensure project benchmarks are being met. As some projects take many years to complete, grant administrators also oversee grant renewal applications. After completion of a project, the grant administrator formally closes the grant.

Depending on the size of the foundation, grant administrators may have other duties. Some train new program officers and grant personnel. They may also be responsible for creating annual grant budgets and foundation reports.

REQUIREMENTS

High School
In high school, take as many classes in business and communications as possible. Coursework in computer science will teach you how to use software and databases.

Postsecondary Training
Educational requirements vary depending on the organization. At smaller foundations, the work may be more administrative in nature—data entry, bookkeeping, and producing reports and brochures. For such positions, potential candidates may get the job without a college degree, but rather on the basis of their past work experience. However, larger foundations require grant administrators to have a bachelor's degree or higher.

It would be beneficial to take coursework in communications, business, and public relations—such classes will give you skills needed to work with many different types of people and organizations. Computer skills will also be important as many foundations rely on grant-making software and databases to code and keep track of their applicants.

Other Requirements

Are you capable of handling many different projects at the same time? You should be a master multitasker in order to succeed in this field. Grant administrators are often assigned numerous applications to evaluate, as well as active grants to monitor. In addition, you may be asked to schedule a field visit and create a report for tomorrow's board meeting. Grant administrators must be efficient, detail oriented, and level headed.

In addition to working well under pressure, grant administrators must be able to communicate well with others—from volunteers and managers of a local charity, to the most prestigious board member.

EXPLORING

To learn more about this career, visit the Web sites of the Grants Managers Network (http://www.gmnetwork.org) and the National Council of Nonprofit Associations (http://www.ncna.org). You should also try to arrange an information interview with a grant administrator about the field. Ask the following questions: What are your primary and secondary job duties? What are your typical work hours? What do you like most and least about your job? How did you train for this field? What advice would you give to young people who are interested in this career?

EMPLOYERS

Foundations are located throughout the United States, providing good prospects for employment in the field. However, most of the larger organizations are located in the "foundation cluster" of metropolitan New York, Washington, D.C., San Francisco, and Los Angeles.

The best opportunities may exist with larger foundations, which have the means for staffing a complete grant administration department. At smaller foundations, these job duties may be handled by individuals in other departments.

STARTING OUT

A job as a *grant assistant* or *program assistant* is a common entry point for this career. Assistants are responsible for creating a file for each grant application, applying the proper code, and keeping track of all correspondence associated with the application. They may also be asked to assemble information needed for the foundation's

Form 990, a required document for the Internal Revenue Service that lists all active grants for the year. Some grant and program assistants may accompany grant administrators on grant follow-up interviews and field visits.

Some individuals may break into this industry by working as *administrative assistants*. Their responsibilities include sending scheduled grant payments, data entry, and assembling reports and documents for board meetings.

ADVANCEMENT

Promotion to *director of grants administration* is the top level of advancement within this career. Directors manage the entire grant administration department including staffing and training. They have more influence during the review process of grant applicants and have final say in how the annual grant budget is allocated.

Some administrators may choose to work for larger foundations with more grant making capabilities. Relocation may be necessary since many of the larger foundation are located in major cities.

EARNINGS

Grant administrators had median annual incomes of $55,000 in 2003, according to the Grants Managers Network. Salary.com reports that grant administrators earned salaries that ranged from less than $41,569 to $84,654 or more in 2007. Most grant administrators receive benefits such as health insurance, retirement plans, savings plans, sick leave, and paid holidays.

WORK ENVIRONMENT

Grant administrators typically work indoors in comfortable, well-lit offices. They use computers to do much of their work, especially when they are evaluating a new grant application. Interviews with potential grantees can be conducted via the phone, but may at times warrant a personal or field visit. Grant administrators may also attend meetings to update board members on the foundation's grant making, provide input on potential grants, and assist with the year's grant budgeting.

OUTLOOK

Employment for grant administrators should be only fair in the next several years due to the limited number of positions available in the field. Turnover is low at large foundations, and grant administration duties may be shared by several staff members at smaller organizations. Opportunities will be best with large organizations in major cities such as Chicago, New York, Los Angeles, San Francisco, and Washington, D.C.

FOR MORE INFORMATION

For information on grant administration, contact the following organizations:

Council on Foundations
1828 L Street, NW, Suite 300
Washington, DC 20036-5104
Tel: 202-466-6512
Email: info@cof.org
http://www.cof.org

Foundation Center
79 Fifth Avenue & 16th Street
New York, NY 10003-3076
Tel: 800-424-9836
http://foundationcenter.org

Grants Managers Network
141 Homestead Avenue
Metairie, LA 70005-3703
Tel: 504-834-9656
Email: info@gmnetwork.org
http://www.gmnetwork.org

National Council of Nonprofit Associations
1101 Vermont Avenue, NW, Suite 1002
Washington, DC 20005-3560
Tel: 202-962-0322
http://www.ncna.org

INTERVIEW

Marissa Camacho Reyes is the executive director of Worldwide Initiatives for Grantmaker Support (http://www.wingsweb.org). She discussed her career with the editors of Careers in Focus: Nonprofit Organizations.

Q. How long have you worked in the nonprofit field?

A. I have been working in the nonprofit sector for the past 32 years. I started as a research assistant in the Philippine Center for Population and Development, a private social development foundation. I stayed in this foundation for 28 years and was its president when I resigned in 2005 to head a newly organized corporate foundation of the biggest fast food chain in the Philippines. After developing the program and getting the Jollibee Foundation off the ground, I resigned in December 2006. I now head the Worldwide Initiatives for Grantmaker Support (WINGS).

Q. Please tell us about your organization.

A. WINGS is a global network of 140 grantmaker associations and support organizations from all regions of the world. Its mission is to strengthen philanthropy and a culture of giving through mutual learning and support, knowledge sharing, and professional development among its members. Why do we consider philanthropy so important? Because we have seen how philanthropy has contributed to improving the welfare and conditions of the poor and marginalized sectors of society in the developing countries as well as pockets of poor communities in developed countries such as the United States.

Q. Why did you decide to enter this field?

A. I was introduced to philanthropy work at a young age. As a young girl, I would accompany my father to his hometown in the province of Bataan, Philippines, every summer and Christmas break. While there my father, who was a lawyer, would offer free legal service to his poor town mates.

My mother was, and still is, an active volunteer in women's clubs, the Red Cross, environmental groups, and other civic groups.

When we were young, my mother used to bring my siblings and me with her to help with various activities in poor communities. These experiences made me realize that there were poor people who did not enjoy the same comforts that my family had. I guess this awareness developed in me the strong desire for public service at a very young age. Since I have no interest to serve the poor through a government position, I chose the nonprofit sector.

Q. What do you like most and least about your job?

A. I get a natural high when I meet individuals and families whose lives have changed for the better because of the opportunities provided by projects or programs I was involved in. I enjoy meeting people from all over the world who are committed to development work because I learn so much from them. My work takes me to different countries and communities, giving me the opportunity to learn about various cultures, see the differences and similarities in development work and meet new friends. Just last month, I met Colombian teenagers, some of whom were former guerrilla fighters, who are trying to rebuild their broken spirit and their lives through dance therapy, counseling, and education services provided by a local foundation.

What I like least about my job is staring poverty in the face, seeing the hopelessness of many people, and knowing that I can only do so much to help solve this social problem.

Q. What are the most important professional qualities for people in your career?

A. It's important to have humility to accept that you don't know everything; that there is something you can learn even from beneficiaries of your programs. You should have integrity and transparency in your work because it is a public trust. Finally, patience is crucial because changes do not happen overnight.

Q. What advice would you give to high school students who are interested in pursuing nonprofit careers?

A. I would advise them to take their social studies classes (or whatever is its equivalent) seriously. They should keep themselves informed about current events, what is happening in their own community, their country, and the rest of the world. Finally, if there are opportunities to volunteer for a community project or interact with the orphans, aged, homeless, poor people, do so.

Grant Coordinators and Writers

OVERVIEW

Grant coordinators are responsible for managing all grant-funded programs for nonprofit organizations. *Grant writers* handle the actual creation and preparation of proposals to potential funders. In smaller organizations, both jobs may be handled by the same person. Both grant coordinators and grant writers may work for schools, local governments, social service agencies, and other organizations to oversee all aspects of grant funding. The Association of Fundraising Professionals reports that it has nearly 28,000 members employed at a variety of nonprofit organizations, including those in the arts, social service, health care, and educational fields, as well as at private consulting firms around the country.

HISTORY

The first recorded government research grant was given to the inventor Samuel Morse in 1842. In the United States, the amount of grants funding has grown consistently and dramatically since that time. More private foundations began bestowing grants when it became clear how much help they could provide to all types of nonprofit groups. Government agencies have increased grants funding, especially in the sciences, recognizing that these grants help U.S. scientists and inventors stay on the cutting edge of new technology.

It is only in the last few decades that the positions of grant coordinator and grant writer have come into being. Organizing and writing grant proposals was usually assigned to various employees (who

48

had other job duties) in each nonprofit agency. Now more and more agencies are recognizing the value of having separate grant coordinators and writers who work solely on grants for the agency.

THE JOB

The number of grants awarded each year in the United States is very large, and so is the competition among grants seekers; hundreds of institutions may apply for the same grant. Furthermore, organizations that award grants have very specific rules and requirements that must be satisfied for a proposal even to be considered.

Grant coordinators must be familiar with all applicable funding organizations and their requirements. They often make the difference in securing the grant for their organizations. Grant coordinators plan and organize all grant-funded programs for their agency or organization. They conduct extensive research on foundations and grant-offering agencies by ordering their publications and contacting officials at the foundations.

To determine which grants the organization should apply for, coordinators work with other officers in their own agency. Grant coordinators participate in many of the planning stages for the agency. For instance, they may sit in on meetings in which budgets are planned and financial officials determine operating budgets, anticipate income, and forecast expenditures. Employees of the nonprofit organization may suggest programs, equipment, or materials that they would like to have funded by a grant, and the grant coordinator determines the best sources of funding for each need.

Before applying for a grant, a grant coordinator maps out a proposal for how the funding would be used. Often these proposals are long and complex. Other employees may help the grant coordinator write up a proposal justifying the need for the program or equipment.

Some nonprofit organizations are fortunate enough to have one or more employees whose primary function is grant writing. In these cases the grant coordinator does not write the grant proposal. The grant writer creates the proposal document, developing its vocabulary and overall structure. Working with the staff whose programs require funding, the grant writer devises a strategy, translating the program to make it relevant to the funder's interests. In the proposal, the grant writer also must communicate both the short-term and long-term goals of the organization so that they are understandable to an outsider. The grant writer also may be responsible for assembling supporting documents that accompany the proposal, such as the organization's budget, board of directors, history, mission, and executive biographies. The grant writer must create different proposals for different kinds of funding, for example, general operating support for the organization overall versus funding for a specific program or project. Additionally, if a grant is received, the grant writer often has to prepare a final report required by many funders.

When an organization does not have a separate grant writer on staff, the writer may be a financial officer in the organization, a teacher in the school, or an employee in charge of a particular project.

Drafts of the proposal usually pass through many hands, including fiscal officers or other executives, before being sent to foundations or grant-offering agencies. Once a final draft has been approved, the grant coordinator or writer prepares the grant proposal using the format required by the funding agency. The proposal then is submitted to the foundation or funding agency. It is the responsibility of the grant coordinator or writer to follow up on the application and meet with agency or foundation representatives if necessary.

Once an organization receives its grant, the coordinator makes sure to meet all of the requirements of the grant-giver. For example, if the grant covers the purchase of equipment, the coordinator confirms receipt of the correct equipment and completes follow-up reports for the foundation or agency. In some instances, the grant coordinator hires an outside agency to monitor the implementation of a grant-funded program. The outside agency then may submit its periodic monitoring reports both to the funding agency and to the grant coordinator.

A large part of the grant coordinator's work involves maintaining files and overseeing paperwork, which is usually done on computer. A thorough grant coordinator must keep the literature published by funding agencies for reference and file copies of all applications and proposals.

Grant coordinators are essentially project managers. They must understand the overall work of their organization while focusing on finding and obtaining the best grants. They see to it that their organization presents itself to funding agencies in the best possible way.

REQUIREMENTS

High School
High school courses in English, journalism, and creative writing will help you develop your written communication skills. Courses in history and the humanities in general also are useful as background reference, and a solid background in mathematics will help you feel comfortable dealing with budgets and other financial documents.

Postsecondary Training

A 2004 survey by the Association of Fundraising Professionals reports that 95.4 percent of respondents held a college degree; of this group, 42 percent held a master's degree or higher. Grant coordinators and writers can have any of several kinds of educational backgrounds. Some study liberal arts, some have business degrees, and some have studied in management training programs.

Regardless of your educational background, you will need the ability to communicate clearly and effectively in writing. Much paperwork is involved in applying for a grant; the funding agency's instructions must be followed precisely, and the proposal must state the institution's goals and objectives in a clear and persuasive way.

Certification or Licensing

The American Grant Writers' Association awards the certified grant writer designation to applicants who complete a four-day workshop. This workshop is designed for grant writers who are employed by nonprofit organizations, religious organizations, schools, and government agencies. Contact the association for more information.

CFRE International offers the certified fund raising executive designation to professionals who meet educational and experience requirements, pass a written examination, and pledge to uphold a code of ethics. This voluntary certification must be renewed every three years. The certification program is administered by CFRE International. Contact the organization for more information.

There is no licensing requirement or specific test that grant coordinators or writers must pass to work in the field.

Other Requirements

Most grant coordinators learn their work on the job. Experience in the workplace helps the coordinator locate the best sources of grants funding and learn the best ways to pursue those sources. For example, if the ideals of a foundation match the intent of the grant coordinator's agency, an ongoing relationship may develop between the agency and the foundation. The grant coordinator learns about these connections in the day-to-day work.

Grant coordinators must have good administrative skills and be detail-oriented. Good communication skills are essential. They work with a wide range of people and must express themselves easily. Coordinators direct and supervise others, so they must be comfortable in management situations. They should be able to influence and persuade others, including their associates and foundation employees. The more grant coordinators and writers understand about the operations of the foundations that they will be applying to, the more successful they will be in writing the grant proposals and securing the requested funding. Grant coordinators and writers must also work well under pressure. There are deadlines to meet, and the responsibility for meeting those deadlines falls squarely on their shoulders. The financial pressure on an organization that does not receive an expected grant can be enormous, and the grant coordinator may bear the responsibility for the loss.

EXPLORING

Volunteering for nonprofit organizations is a good way to find out about a grant coordinator's work firsthand. Contact local religious organizations, charities, health organizations, or social service agencies. In nonprofit organizations that have grant coordinators, the ideal internship or volunteer experience involves assisting with a grant application project. Sometimes schools have their own grant application projects several times a year. You can get an understanding of all of the work involved by seeing the application or proposal process through from start to finish.

Several organizations sponsor intensive workshops on grant coordination and fund-raising. The Grantsmanship Center (http://www.tgci.com) conducts seminars and workshops in cities across the United States 150 times a year. It helps grant coordinators and writers with proposal writing and other aspects of their jobs. Its publication, *Grantsmanship Center Magazine,* and the guide, *Program Planning and Proposal Writing,* are good resources for grant writers and coordinators. The Grantsmanship Center also maintains a reference library. Many fund-raising organizations also have helpful publications for the potential grant coordinator. An annual almanac, *Giving USA* is published by the Giving USA Foundation (http://www.aafrc.com).

Some colleges and universities offer courses in fund-raising. These may even include business lectures or seminars on the grant application process. Many colleges also offer courses in arts management or in nonprofit work that would help potential grant coordinators and writers understand the type of work required in this occupation.

EMPLOYERS

Grant writers and coordinators work for nonprofit organizations and agencies, such as social service agencies, arts organizations, museums, educational institutions, and research foundations. Grant writers also work independently as freelancers. They contract their services to smaller nonprofit agencies or individuals who might seek funding for an arts program or a scientific research project, for example.

STARTING OUT

After earning your bachelor's degree, apply for a job at a nonprofit organization. Keep in mind that you will probably be hired by an agency to do tasks other than grant writing or coordinating. You first need to learn how the organization operates and understand its goals before beginning to work with grants. In these first years, many prospective coordinators and writers sign up for management training programs or courses in technical writing, psychology, sociology, and statistical methods.

ADVANCEMENT

Since grant coordinators almost always begin their careers in other work, they advance into grant positions by showing an understanding of the organization's goals. Once the organization moves a person into a grant position, advancement comes with successful work on grant proposals and obtaining the necessary funding. If the grant coordina-

Did You Know?

- About 1.4 million nonprofit organizations are registered (most as "public charities") with the Internal Revenue Service.
- California (34,000) has the highest number of public charities and Wyoming and North Dakota have the fewest (1,000 each).
- Human service organizations (35 percent) are the most common type of public charity, followed by education (18 percent), health care (13 percent), public and societal benefit (12 percent), and arts, culture, and humanities (11 percent).
- Approximately 13 million people in the United States work for nonprofit organizations.
- The nonprofit sector accounts for 8.3 percent of wages and salaries paid in the United States.
- The nonprofit sector of the U.S. economy has employment growth of approximately 2.5 percent a year—higher than the employment growth for the for-profit business and government sectors of the economy.
- Approximately 61.2 million people in the United States were active volunteers between September 2005 and September 2006. Nearly 75 percent of volunteers worked for nonprofit organizations.

Source: U.S. Department of Labor, Independent Sector, *Nonprofit Almanac 2007*

tor and writer positions are separate, usually grant writers advance to grant coordinators, having gained expertise and familiarity with the funding community. But because nonprofit organizations often employ only one person responsible for grant writing and coordination, a grant administrator advances by moving into a position with a larger nonprofit organization that requires higher-level skills.

EARNINGS

According to *Compensation in Nonprofit Organizations 2006*, a report from Abbott, Langer & Associates, grant writers had median annual incomes of $35,875 in 2006. The average salaries of surveyed members of the Association of Fundraising Professionals were much higher, at $71,305 a year in 2006. The salary survey noted that earnings varied among members based on position, organization, location, and experience. Pay differences based on gender and ethnic background were also discovered.

Freelance grant coordinators usually charge separate fees for research and grant writing.

Benefits for grant coordinators and writers often are equivalent to other professional business positions, including paid vacation, group insurance plans, and paid sick days.

WORK ENVIRONMENT

Grant coordinators work primarily in comfortable office environments. Some nonprofit agencies have cramped or inadequate facilities, while others may be quite luxurious. The grant coordinator usually works during regular office hours unless a deadline must be met. When grant coordinators approach the deadlines for submitting grant proposals, overtime work, including nights or weekends, may be required. Meetings with foundation representatives may take place outside the office or before or after regular hours. Benefits packages and vacation time vary widely from agency to agency, but most nonprofit organizations are flexible places to work. Grant coordinators are often most satisfied with their jobs when they believe in the goals of their own agency and know they are helping the agency do its work.

OUTLOOK

The outlook for grant coordinators and writers is steady. Although overall giving has increased over the last several years, hundreds of agencies are applying for the same grants—which has resulted in strong competition for funding. A top grant coordinator or writer can make the difference between the organization that gets the funding and the one that does not. A grant coordinator who has proven success in coordinating grants proposals and obtaining grants, as well as a grant writer who has written successful proposals, should be able to find work. Many people who work in nonprofit organizations believe that more grant coordinators and writers will be hired as more of these organizations realize that a professional grant administrator may help them get funding they have been missing. The grant coordinator's knowledge of how to choose the most appropriate sources of grant funding and implement funding programs is invaluable to nonprofit organizations.

FOR MORE INFORMATION

For information on certification, contact
American Grant Writers' Association
PO Box 8481
Seminole, FL 33775-8481
Tel: 727-366-9334
Email: customerservice@agwa.us
http://www.agwa.us

For information on fund-raising careers, educational programs, and other resources, contact
Association of Fundraising Professionals
4300 Wilson Boulevard, Suite 300
Arlington, VA 22203-4179
Tel: 703-684-0410
http://www.afpnet.org

For information on certification as a certified fund raising executive, contact
CFRE International
4900 Seminary Road, Suite 670
Alexandria, VA 22311-1811
Tel: 703-820-5555
Email: info@cfre.org
http://www.cfre.org

This organization is a coalition of consulting firms working in the nonprofit sector.
Giving Institute: Leading Consultants to Non-Profits
4700 West Lake Avenue
Glenview, IL 60025-1468

Tel: 800-462-2372
Email: info@givinginstitute.org
http://www.aafrc.org

The following organization provides assistance on proposal writing, offers 150 seminars annually, and publishes Grantsmanship Center Magazine:

The Grantsmanship Center
PO Box 17220
Los Angeles, CA 90017-0220
Tel: 213-482-9860
Email: info@tgci.com
http://www.tgci.com

HIV/AIDS Counselors and Case Managers

OVERVIEW

HIV/AIDS counselors and case managers work with people who are infected with HIV (human immunodeficiency virus) or have developed AIDS (acquired immunodeficiency syndrome), and with their families and friends, to help them cope with the physical and emotional results of the disease. They answer questions, offer advice and support, and help HIV/AIDS patients get necessary assistance from medical and social agencies.

HISTORY

No one knows the exact origin of HIV, though there are several different theories. The virus has existed in the United States, Haiti, and Africa since at least 1977 or 1978. In 1979, doctors in Los Angeles and New York began to diagnose and report rare types of pneumonia, cancer, and other illnesses not usually found in persons with healthy immune systems.

The Centers for Disease Control and Prevention (CDC) officially named the condition AIDS in 1982. In 1984, the virus responsible for weakening the immune system was identified as HIV.

Today, the CDC estimates that more than 1 million Americans are living with HIV, and approximately 40,000 new infections occur each year. The professions of HIV/AIDS counselor and case manager developed in the mid-1980s as a division of social work.

THE JOB

HIV/AIDS counselors and case managers help HIV and AIDS patients deal with their illness in the best way possible. A person who has tested positive for HIV or who has been diagnosed as having AIDS has many issues to deal with. Some of the issues are similar to those faced by anyone diagnosed with a terminal illness—grief, fear, and concerns over health care, financial planning, and making provisions for children or other family members. Other issues these patients may face are unique to HIV and AIDS sufferers. These may include discrimination, prejudice, and exclusion by family and acquaintances who are afraid of, or do not understand, the disease. Another special consideration for these patients is how to avoid passing the disease on to others.

Counselors and case managers offer support and assistance in dealing with all the various social, physical, and emotional issues patients face. Together counselors and case managers work with clients in all stages of the disease—from those who have first tested positive for HIV to those who are in the final stages of the illness. They may work at HIV testing centers, public health clinics, mental health clinics, family planning clinics, hospitals, and drug treatment facilities.

Counselors who work at testing facilities, sometimes called *test counselors,* work with individuals who are being tested for HIV. These counselors usually meet with clients before they are tested to find out about the client's level of risk for the disease, to explain the testing procedure, and to talk about what the possible test results mean. They also explain how the HIV infection is spread, discuss ways to prevent it, and answer general questions about the disease and its progress.

Results from the test are typically available a few days to two weeks after the client has had the initial meeting. When the client returns to find out the results, the counselor again meets with him or her. If the results are negative, the counselor may suggest re-testing if, during the six months before the test, the client engaged in any behaviors that might have resulted in infection. Since the infection does not show up immediately after it is contracted, it is possible to be infected and still test negative.

If the results are positive, the counselor talks with the client about his or her sexual activity and drug use to determine how they might have gotten the disease. They also help them decide whom to notify of the test results, such as previous sex partners.

At some testing clinics, such as those offering STD (sexually transmitted disease) testing as well as HIV testing, a client initially meets with a nurse who conducts the test. In these circumstances, when the client returns for the test results he or she may then meet with an HIV counselor if necessary.

The counselor is often the first person the HIV-positive client talks to about the illness. A large part of the job, then, is referring the client to appropriate sources of help, including AIDS-related agencies, social services, and health care providers.

Case managers, unlike counselors, follow patients through the various stages of their illness, helping them coordinate and manage the resources necessary to deal with it. In some instances, case managers may not begin working with a client until that client has developed AIDS. Through letters, phone calls, and contacts with a network of available service providers, case managers help their clients get access to the agencies or organizations that offer the assistance they need. Assistance may include medical care, legal help, help with living expenses, or visits by home health care aides.

People with HIV and AIDS are under severe emotional strain. In addition to coping with the physical effects of the disease, they must also cope with the burden of having a disease that much of society does not understand or accept. They may feel anger, depression, guilt, and shame as they learn to live with their disease.

Counselors and case managers help clients deal with these emotional strains. They may conduct AIDS support groups or group counseling sessions in which HIV or AIDS patients discuss their experiences and questions about living with the disease. In these group sessions, the counselor or case manager oversees the conversation and tries to move it in a positive direction.

HIV/AIDS counselors and case managers may also work with the family members, friends, and partners of those with HIV or AIDS, either in individual or group sessions. They may meet with family members or partners to discuss the client's progress or to help them understand their loved one's needs. They may also set up and oversee grief counseling sessions for those who have lost relatives or partners to the disease.

In order to monitor clients' progress, case managers keep written records on each of their sessions. They may be required to participate in staff meetings to discuss a client's progress and treatment plan. They may also meet with members of various social service agencies to discuss their clients' needs.

In addition to the primary duty of counseling clients, these workers may participate in community efforts to increase HIV and AIDS awareness. They may help develop workshops, give speeches to high schools or other groups, or organize and lead public awareness campaigns.

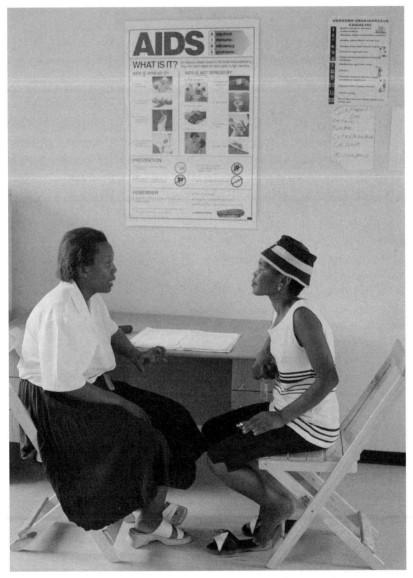

A counselor at an AIDS clinic talks to a patient who is undergoing an anti-retroviral treatment. *(Gideon Mendel, Corbis)*

REQUIREMENTS

High School

If you are considering a career in the field of HIV/AIDS counseling, you should emphasize sociology and psychology classes in your curriculum. Because this area of counseling requires an understanding of how the human body is affected by HIV and AIDS, you should also take classes such as biology, physiology, and health. To develop your communication skills, take English classes. You may also want to take a foreign language, which will give you the ability to communicate with non-English speakers.

Postsecondary Training

Although specific educational requirements for HIV/AIDS counselors and case managers vary, most employers require a bachelor's degree in mental health, counseling, or social work. Some employers may require their employees to have a master's degree. A college-level curriculum for a degree in mental health or social work is likely to include classes in counseling, sociology, psychology, human development, and mental health. Your college education will also include a minimum of 400 hours of supervised field work, known as a practicum. The Council on Social Work Education (CSWE) is the only accrediting body for bachelor's and master's degree programs in social work in the United States. When selecting a program to attend, make sure it is CSWE approved. To view a listing of such programs, go to the Accredited Programs section of the CSWE's Web site, http://www .cswe.org. You can also order the print version, *Directory of Colleges and Universities with Accredited Social Work Degree Programs*. The master's degree in social work allows you to concentrate your studies on your field of practice. These programs usually last two to two and a half years and require supervised fieldwork of at least 900 hours.

Some employers will hire job candidates with bachelor's degrees in other fields, such as education. To prepare yourself for this work, however, you should include such classes as psychology and health in your course work. Gaining work experience will be essential for you, so look for internships or summer jobs that offer the opportunity to combine your interests, for example in public health education or with an HIV/AIDS service organization. If you cannot find a paid position, you can still strengthen your resume by doing volunteer work at an HIV/AIDS organization; many are involved in such areas as advocacy, education, and home support services.

Certification or Licensing

Most states require some form of credentialing for HIV/AIDS counselors and case managers. Many choose to be certified by the National Board for Certified Counselors (NBCC). To become certified by the NBCC, candidates must have completed a master's degree in counseling, have at least two years of professional experience, and pass a national examination. Upon successful completion of these requirements, the candidate is designated as a national certified counselor. Additionally, all states require some form of licensing, registration, or certification for anyone working as a social worker. Requirements vary by state, so you will need to check with your state's licensing board for specific information.

Other Requirements

Because these diseases receive so much attention from the medical, social, and even government arenas, there are often new developments in HIV- and AIDS-related treatments, policies, and services. In order to keep up-to-date, counselors and case managers must regularly continue their education by attending seminars or monthly in-service meetings.

For individuals considering a career in HIV/AIDS counseling, certain personal qualifications may be just as important as having the correct educational background. Compassion, sensitivity, and the desire to help others are key qualities for these counselors. They must also be able to communicate effectively and sincerely and to listen with understanding.

HIV/AIDS counselors and case managers must be emotionally stable and resilient in order to keep from becoming depressed and discouraged by the nature of their work. They need to be able to avoid becoming too emotionally involved with their patients by balancing empathy with objectivity.

EXPLORING

If you are interested in a career in HIV/AIDS counseling, you might contact local hospitals, HIV testing centers, or AIDS service organizations for more information. It may be possible to meet with a counselor to talk about the details of his or her job. Any school or local library should also have a large number of resources both on the AIDS virus and on counseling. You can also use the Internet to get the latest information about HIV and AIDS by visiting such sources as the CDC (http://www.cdc.gov) and the HIV/AIDS Bureau of the Health Resources and Services Administration (http://www.hab.hrsa.gov).

To further explore the career, you may be able to find a volunteer position in a social service agency, health clinic, or hospital. Even if the position does not deal directly with HIV or AIDS patients, it should provide you with an idea of what it is like to work in such an environment. Once you have graduated from high school, you may be eligible to join the National AIDS Fund AmeriCorps/Caring Counts Program, which trains participants to do HIV/AIDS education and counseling and places them in selected cities for approximately 11 months of service. (See the end of this article for the fund's contact information.)

HIV/AIDS Statistics

The Centers for Disease Control reports the following HIV/AIDS statistics as of the end of 2005:

- The cumulative number of AIDS cases in the United States was 952,629, including 815,488 adult males and 126,964 adult females. There were 10,177 AIDS cases reported in children under the age of 15.
- Total deaths of persons reported with AIDS were 550,394, including 525,442 adults and adolescents (children 13 and above).

The Joint United Nations Programme on HIV/AIDS reports the following worldwide trends as of the end of 2006:

- Approximately 39.5 million people worldwide were living with HIV/AIDS (19.5 million men, 17.7 million women, and 2.3 million children under the age of 15).
- Sub-Saharan Africa (24.7 million) and South and Southeast Asia (7.8 million) had the largest number of people living with HIV/AIDS.
- During 2006, AIDS caused the deaths of an estimated 2.9 million people (2.6 million adults and 380,000 children under the age of 15).
- In 2006, approximately 4.3 million people acquired the human immunodeficiency virus (HIV).

EMPLOYERS

HIV/AIDS counselors and case managers work for hospitals, hospices, HIV testing centers, public health clinics, mental health clinics, social service agencies, Red Cross offices, Planned Parenthood centers, and various AIDS service organizations. They may also work for regional AIDS consortia organized by health officials, religious leaders, educators, business leaders, and AIDS service representatives.

STARTING OUT

New graduates may begin their job searches at the career services centers of their colleges. They might also apply directly to any area social service, health, or AIDS service organizations. Some openings for HIV/AIDS counselors or case managers might be advertised in the classified sections of local newspapers. Membership in a professional organization, such as the American Counseling Association, might also provide the job seeker with leads through publications, meetings, or job banks. Additionally, graduates may look for internship opportunities, such as the University of California-San Francisco AIDS Health Project's Post-Baccalaureate Internship Program. This year-long program offers new college graduates focused education and experience in HIV care. Through such internships, graduates can hone professional skills as well as make professional contacts that may lead to later full-time employment.

ADVANCEMENT

Counselors and case managers who work for large organizations will have more opportunity for advancement than those who work for smaller ones. In a large organization, for example, the counselor with education and experience might move into an administrative position, such as senior trainer or program director. Because smaller organizations, especially not-for-profit organizations, usually have small staffs, advancement is often slow and limited.

Those who continue their education may have a wider range of possibilities for advancement. Counselors who complete a master's degree in social work or rehabilitative counseling, for example, might be employed by social welfare agencies as medical or psychiatric social workers, child protective workers, rehabilitative counselors, or parole or probation officers. These fields have a broader scope of advancement opportunities.

Finally, some who continue their education elect to go into research or teaching at the college level.

EARNINGS

Generally, earnings for HIV/AIDS counselors and case managers are similar to those for other counselors and social workers. Salaries can vary, however, depending upon the experience and education of the individual and the location, size, and funding source of the employer. The U.S. Department of Labor reported the median yearly earnings of mental and public health social workers as $43,040 in 2006. The lowest paid 10 percent made less than $27,280 per year, while the highest paid 10 percent earned more than $64,070. Those at the top end of the pay scale typically have extensive experience and advanced degrees and work at well-funded programs.

In addition to salary, most HIV/AIDS counselors and case managers receive a benefits package that includes paid vacations, holidays, and sick time, medical insurance, and sometimes a retirement plan.

WORK ENVIRONMENT

HIV/AIDS counselors and case managers usually work regular eight-hour days, five days a week. Occasionally, however, they may have appointments with health care providers, social service agencies, or patients outside of regular office hours.

Counselors who work in HIV testing centers and health clinics usually have on-site offices where they can talk privately with clients. Those who work as case managers may visit clients in their homes or in hospitals or other long-range care facilities. They may conduct group sessions in classrooms or conference rooms of hospitals or social service agencies. Regardless of the setting, HIV/AIDS counselors and case managers spend a majority of their day meeting with people—either clients and family members or representatives from social service or health care agencies.

Counseling those with HIV and AIDS is stressful and often depressing work. In most cases, clients are preparing for eventual death, and they turn to the counseling professional for help and support in facing it. Case managers often watch their clients become very sick as the virus progresses; frequently, they must deal with clients' deaths. Dealing with this sickness, death, and the accompanying emotional distress on a daily basis may be difficult.

OUTLOOK

Employment trends for HIV/AIDS counselors and case managers are likely to depend upon government funding for AIDS-related programs, since private funding for such programs is usually limited. Government funding for health programs, however, fluctuates, and resistance from some special interest groups or policy makers may negatively influence spending on AIDS research and programs. Nevertheless, the U.S. Department of Labor predicts that employment for social workers, who are closely related professionals, will grow faster than the average for all occupations through 2014. Additional factors influencing job opportunities for HIV/AIDS counselors and case managers include the continued spread of HIV, the increased number of people living longer with HIV than in previous years, and the new complications (medical, financial, and even social) that are brought on by new treatments. Given all of these various factors, experts predict the employment outlook for HIV/AIDS counselors to be on the increase.

These professionals can play an especially important role in educating the public at large and those with HIV and AIDS on how to cope with the disease and avoid its spread. Jobs for HIV/AIDS counselors and case managers will probably be most plentiful in urban areas, with their larger populations. Those with the most current knowledge and HIV/AIDS training will find the best opportunities.

FOR MORE INFORMATION

For information about counseling and graduate programs in counseling, contact
American Counseling Association
5999 Stevenson Avenue
Alexandria, VA 22304-3304
Tel: 800-347-6647
http://www.counseling.org

For information about HIV and AIDS, contact the following organizations:
Centers for Disease Control and Prevention
1600 Clifton Road
Atlanta, GA 30329-4018
Tel: 404-639-3311
http://www.cdc.gov

HIV/AIDS Bureau
U.S. Department of Health and Human Services
Health Resources and Services Administration
5600 Fishers Lane
Rockville, MD 20857-0001
Tel: 301-443-3376
http://www.hab.hrsa.gov

For information on social work careers, contact
National Association of Social Workers
750 First Street, NE, Suite 700
Washington, DC 20002-4241
Tel: 202-408-8600
http://www.naswdc.org

For information on certification, contact
National Board for Certified Counselors
Three Terrace Way
Greensboro, NC 27403-3660
Tel: 336-547-0607
Email: nbcc@nbcc.org
http://www.nbcc.org

For more information on this AmeriCorps program, contact
National AIDS Fund AmeriCorps/Caring Counts Program
729 15th Street, NW, 9th Floor
Washington, DC 20005-1511
Tel: 888-234-2437
Email: info@aidsfund.org
http://www.aidsfund.org

Human Services Workers

QUICK FACTS

School Subjects
Health
Sociology

Personal Skills
Communication/ideas
Helping/teaching

Work Environment
Primarily indoors
Primarily one location

Minimum Education Level
Some postsecondary training

Salary Range
$16,180 to $25,580 to
$40,780+

Certification or Licensing
None available

Outlook
Much faster than the average

DOT
195

GOE
12.02.02

NOC
4212

O*NET-SOC
21-1093.00

OVERVIEW

Under the supervision of social workers, psychologists, sociologists, and other professionals, *human services workers* offer support to families, the elderly, the poor, and others in need. They teach life and communication skills to people in mental health facilities or substance abuse programs. Employed by agencies, shelters, halfway houses, and hospitals, they work individually with clients or in group counseling. They also direct clients to social services and benefits. There are approximately 352,000 human services workers employed in the United States.

HISTORY

Before the 20th century, charity and philanthropy consisted mainly of donations from the affluent. These donations were distributed by church groups to the needy. No systematic methods were established to follow up on charity cases or improve the conditions of the poor in any permanent way.

After the industrial revolution, public opinion about the inequities of wealth began to change. In 1889, Jane Addams, the daughter of a banker, founded Hull House in Chicago, an act that is usually considered the birth of formal social work. Addams's philosophy of helping the under-privileged gain a better, more permanent standard of living inspired many others to launch similar programs in other parts of the world. After World War I, social work began to be recognized as a valid career. The Great Depression of the 1930s provided further impetus to the growth of social work, as the federal government joined with state, municipal, and private efforts to ease the pain of poverty. The social disruptions of the years following World War II contributed to further growth in social work. Today, social workers and human services workers are employed in a variety of institutional and community settings, administering help and support to the poor, the homeless, the aged, the disabled and mentally ill, substance abusers, parolees, and others having trouble with adjustments in life.

THE JOB

The term "human services" covers a wide range of careers, from counseling prison inmates to counseling the families of murder victims; from helping someone with a disability find a job to caring for the child of a teenage mother during the school day. From one-on-one interaction to group interaction, from paperwork to footwork, the human services worker is focused on improving the lives of others.

As society changes, so do the concerns of human services workers. New societal problems (such as the rapid spread of AIDS among teenagers and the threat of gang violence) require special attention, as do changes in the population (such as the increasing number of elderly people living on their own and the increasing number of minimum-wage workers unable to fully provide for their families). New laws and political movements also affect human services workers because many social service programs rely heavily on federal and state aid. Although government policy makers are better educated than the policy makers of years past, social service programs are more threatened than ever before. Despite all these changes in society and the changes in the theories of social work, some things stay the same—human services workers care about the well-being of individuals and communities. They are sensitive to the needs of diverse groups of people, and they are actively involved in meeting the needs of the public.

Human services workers have had many of the same responsibilities throughout the years. They offer their clients counseling, representation, emotional support, and the services they need. Although some human services workers assist professionals with the development and evaluation of social programs, policy analysis, and other administrative duties, most work directly with clients.

This direct work can involve aid to specific populations, such as ethnic groups, women, and the poor. Many human services workers assist poor people in numerous ways. They interview clients to identify needed services. They care for clients' children during job or medical appointments and offer clients emotional support. They determine whether clients are eligible for food stamps, Medicaid, or other welfare programs. In some food stamp programs, aides advise low-income family members how to plan, budget, shop for, and prepare balanced meals, often accompanying or driving clients to the store and offering suggestions on the most nutritious and economical food to purchase.

Some aides serve tenants in public housing projects. They are employed by housing agencies or other groups to help tenants relocate. They inform tenants of the use of facilities and the location of community services, such as recreation centers and clinics. They also explain the management's rules about sanitation and maintenance. They may at times help resolve disagreements between tenants and landlords.

Members of specific populations call on the aid of human services workers for support, information, and representation. The human services worker can provide these clients with counseling and emotional support and direct them to support groups and services. Social workers work with human services workers to reach out to the people; together, they visit individuals, families, and neighborhood groups to publicize the supportive services available.

Other clients of human services workers are those experiencing life-cycle changes. Children, adolescents, and the elderly may require assistance in making transitions. Human services workers help parents find proper day care for their children. They educate young mothers about how to care for an infant. They counsel children struggling with family problems or peer pressure. They offer emotional support to gay, lesbian, and bisexual teenagers and involve them in support groups. Some programs help the elderly stay active and help them prepare meals and clean their homes. They also assist the elderly in getting to and from hospitals and community centers and stay in touch with these clients through home visits and telephone calls.

Some human services workers focus on specific problems, such as drug and alcohol abuse. Human services workers assist in developing, organizing, and conducting programs dealing with the causes of and remedies for substance abuse. Workers may help individuals trying to overcome drug or alcohol addiction to master practical skills, such as cooking and doing laundry, and teach them ways to communicate more effectively with others. Domestic violence is also a problem receiving more attention, as more and more people leave abusive situations. Shelters for victims require counselors, assistants, tutors, and day care personnel for their children. Human services workers may also teach living and communication skills in homeless shelters and mental health facilities.

Record keeping is an important part of the duties of human services workers, because records may affect a client's eligibility for future benefits, the proper assessment of a program's success, and the prospect of future funding. Workers prepare and maintain records and case files of every person with whom they work. They record clients' responses to the various programs and treatment. They must also track costs in group homes in order to stay within budget.

Career Options for Those with a Degree in Human Services

Students who earn a degree in human services have a wealth of options available to them. Here a just a few of the options available to graduates, according to the U.S. Department of Labor.

- Adult Day Care Worker
- Alcohol Counselor
- Assistant Case Manager
- Behavioral Management Aide
- Case Management Aide
- Case Monitor
- Case Worker
- Child Abuse Worker
- Child Advocate
- Client Advocate
- Community Action Worker
- Community Organizer
- Community Outreach Worker
- Crisis Intervention Counselor
- Drug Abuse Counselor
- Eligibility Counselor
- Family Support Worker
- Gerontology Aide
- Group Activities Aide
- Group Home Worker
- Halfway House Counselor
- Home Health Aide
- Intake Interviewer
- Juvenile Court Liaison
- Life Skills Instructor
- Mental Health Aide
- Neighborhood Worker
- Parole Officer
- Probation Officer
- Psychological Aide
- Rehabilitation Case Worker
- Residential Counselor
- Residential Manager
- Social Service Aide
- Social Service Liaison
- Social Service Technician
- Social Work Assistant
- Therapeutic Assistant
- Youth Worker

REQUIREMENTS

High School

Some employers hire people with only a high school education, but these employees might find it hard to move beyond clerical positions. Interested high school students should plan to attend a college or university and should take classes in English, mathematics, political science, psychology, and sociology.

Postsecondary Training

Certificate and associate's degree programs in human services or mental health are offered at community and junior colleges, vocational-technical institutes, and other postsecondary institutions. It is also possible to pursue a bachelor's degree in human services. Almost 500 human services education programs exist; academic programs such as these prepare students for occupations in the human services. Because the educators at these colleges and universities stay in regular contact with the social work employers in their area, the programs are continually revised to meet the changing needs of the field. Students are exposed early and often to the kinds of situations they may encounter on the job.

Undergraduate and graduate programs typically include courses in psychology, sociology, crisis intervention, family dynamics, therapeutic interviewing, rehabilitation, and gerontology.

Other Requirements

Many people perform human services work because they want to make a difference in their community. They may also like connecting on a personal level with other people, offering them emotional support, helping them sort out problems, and teaching them how to care for themselves and their families. A genuine interest in the lives and concerns of others and a sensitivity to their situations are important to a human services worker. An artistic background can also be valuable in human services. Some programs in mental health facilities, domestic violence shelters, and other group homes use art therapy. Painting, music, dance, and creative writing are sometimes incorporated into counseling sessions, providing a client with alternative modes of expression.

In addition to the rewarding aspects of the job, a human services worker must be prepared to take on difficult responsibilities. The work can be very stressful. The problems of some populations—such as prison inmates, battered women and children, substance abusers, and the poor—can seem insurmountable. Their stories and day-to-day lives can seem tragic. Even if human services workers are

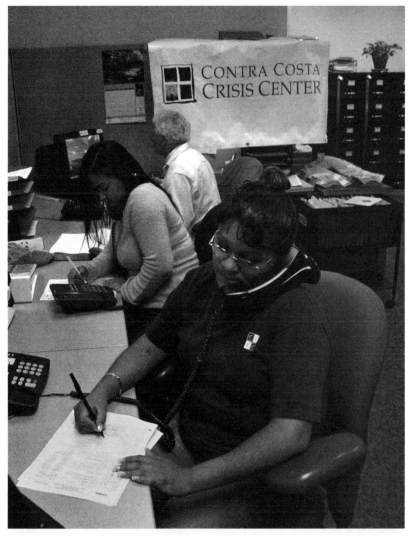

Human services workers answer phones in a crisis center. Callers may be fighting drug or alcohol abuse, contemplating suicide, or facing domestic abuse. *(Geri Engberg, The Image Works)*

not counseling clients, they are working directly with clients on some level. Just helping a person fill out an application or prepare a household budget requires a good disposition and the ability to be supportive. Clients may not welcome help and may not even care about their own well-being. In these cases, a human services worker must remain firm but supportive and encouraging. Patience is very important, whatever the area of human service.

The workload for a human services worker can also be overwhelming. An agency with limited funding cannot always afford to hire the number of employees it needs. A human services worker employed by an understaffed agency will probably be overworked. This can sometimes result in employee burnout.

EXPLORING

To get an idea of the requirements of human service, you can volunteer your time to a local human services agency or institution. Religious organizations also involve young people in volunteer work, as do the Red Cross, the Boy Scouts, and the Girl Scouts. Volunteer work could include reading to blind or elderly people and visiting nursing homes and halfway homes. You might get involved organizing group recreation programs at the YMCA or YWCA or performing light clerical duties in an office. You could also encourage any high school organizations to which you belong to become actively involved in charity work.

Some members of high school organizations also perform social services within their own schools, educating classmates on the dangers of gangs, unsafe sex, and substance abuse. By being actively involved in your community, you can gain experience in human services as well as build up a history of volunteer service that will impress future employers.

EMPLOYERS

Approximately 352,000 human services workers are employed in the United States. They are employed in a variety of settings, including agency offices, community centers, group homes, halfway houses, mental health facilities, hospitals, shelters, and the private homes of clients.

STARTING OUT

Students may find jobs through their high school counselors or local and state human services agencies. Sometimes summer jobs and volunteer work can develop into full-time employment upon graduation. Employers try to be selective in their hiring because many human services jobs involve direct contact with people who are impaired and therefore vulnerable to exploitation. Experience with helping others is a definite advantage.

ADVANCEMENT

Job performance has some bearing on pay raises and advancement for human services workers. However, career advancement almost always depends on formal education, such as a bachelor's or master's degree in social work, counseling, rehabilitation, or some other related field. Many employers encourage their workers to further their education and some may even reimburse part of the costs of school. In addition, many employers provide in-service training such as seminars and workshops.

EARNINGS

Salaries of human services workers depend in part on their employer and amount of experience. According to the U.S. Department of Labor, median annual earnings of social and human service assistants were $25,580 in 2006. Salaries ranged from less than $16,180 to more than $40,780.

Benefit for full-time workers include vacation and sick time, health (and sometimes dental) insurance, and pension or 401(k) plans.

WORK ENVIRONMENT

Most human services professionals work a standard 40-hour week, spending time both in the office and in the field interviewing clients and performing other support services. Some weekend and evening work may be required, but compensatory time off is usually granted. Workers in residential settings generally work in shifts. Because group homes need 24-hour staffing, workers usually work some evenings and weekends.

Work conditions are affected by the size and location of the town in which the work is found. The societal problems of large, urban areas are different from those of small, rural areas. In a city, human services workers deal with issues of crime, racism, gang warfare, and violence in the schools. These problems can exist in smaller communities as well, but human services workers in rural areas focus more on work with the elderly and the poor. Rural communities typically have an older population, with people living deeper in the country and farther from public and private services. This can require more transportation time. The social services in rural areas, because of lower salaries and poorer facilities, typically have trouble attracting workers.

Offices and facilities may be clean and cheerful, or they may be dismal, cramped, and inadequately equipped. While out in the field with clients, workers may also find themselves in dangerous, squalid areas. In a large city, workers can rely on public transportation, whereas workers in a rural community must often drive long distances.

OUTLOOK

Employment for human services workers will grow much faster than the average for all occupations through 2014, according to the U.S. Department of Labor. The best opportunities will be in job-training programs, residential care facilities, and private social service agencies, which include such services as adult day care and meal delivery programs. Correctional facilities are also expected to employ many more human services workers. Because counseling inmates and offenders can be undesirable work, there are a number of high-paying jobs available in that area.

New ideas in treating people with disabilities or mental illness also influence employment growth in group homes and residential care facilities. Public concern for the homeless—many of whom are former mental patients who were released under service reductions in the 1980s—as well as for troubled teenagers, and those with substance abuse problems, is likely to bring about new community-based programs and group residences.

Job prospects in public agencies are not as bright as they once were because of fiscal policies that tighten eligibility requirements for federal welfare and other payments. State and local governments are expected to remain major employers, however, as the burden of providing social services such as welfare, child support, and nutrition programs is shifted from the federal government to the state and local level. In larger cities, such as New York or Washington, D.C., jobs in the public sector will be more plentiful than in smaller cities because of the higher demand. There is also a higher burnout rate in the larger cities, resulting in more job opportunities as people vacate their positions for other careers.

FOR MORE INFORMATION

For more information on careers in counseling, contact
American Counseling Association
5999 Stevenson Avenue
Alexandria, VA 22304-3304
Tel: 800-347-6647
http://www.counseling.org

To access the online publication Choices: Careers in Social Work, *visit the NASW's Web site.*
National Association of Social Workers (NASW)
750 First Street, NE, Suite 700
Washington, DC 20002-4241
Tel: 202-408-8600
http://www.naswdc.org

For information on student memberships, scholarships, and master's degree programs in human services, visit the NOHS's Web site.
National Organization for Human Services (NOHS)
90 Madison Street, Suite 206
Denver, CO 80206-5418
Tel: 303-320-5430
http://www.nationalhumanservices.org

For information on employment with government human services agencies, contact
U.S. Department of Health and Human Services
200 Independence Avenue, SW
Washington, DC 20201-0004
Tel: 877-696-6775
http://www.hhs.gov

The following is a job search Web site for social services and social work positions:
SocialService.Com
http://www.socialservice.com

INTERVIEW

Mary Grant is a case manager for a nonprofit organization that provides specialized services for people with mental retardation and developmental disabilities such as cerebral palsy, autism, and epilepsy. She discussed her career with the editors of Careers in Focus: Nonprofit Organizations.

Q. Please tell us about your work.
A. I coordinate services for adults with developmental disabilities in such areas as physical therapy, occupational therapy, speech therapy, psychological and psychiatric care, general medical health care, academic skills, daily living skills, vocational train-

ing, and day and residential services. I have been a case manager for more than three years.

Q. Why did you decide to become a case manager?

A. I was already working in the field as a developmental training supervisor, and I wanted to take on more responsibility; it was a good opportunity for professional growth and advancement.

Q. What type of educational path did you pursue to become a case manager?

A. I have a bachelor of arts in psychology. Most employers require a bachelor's degree in social work, psychology, or another human services-related discipline, and at least one year of experience working with individuals with developmental disabilities.

Q. What do you like most and least about your job?

A. Most: Being a case manager can be very rewarding. Directly interacting with the adults on my caseload, seeing them learn new skills, gain confidence, and sometimes even improve their health—basically, just knowing that you are helping someone reach their potential.

Least: Being a case manager can be very stressful. There is a lot to juggle, between keeping up with the paperwork, coordinating appointments with one or more professionals, having to react if someone on your caseload has a medical emergency, or intervening if they are having problems. Also, this type of position usually does not command a high salary—you have to be in this field because you love what you do.

Q. What are the three most important professional qualities for case managers?

A. It's hard to say, because a case manager has to do so many different things. Overall, I would say patience—it will be tested on a daily basis; flexibility—the ability to roll with the punches, because people are unpredictable and nothing ever goes as planned; and organizational skills—they are also a must, as you need to juggle myriad professional services, goals, and licensing requirements with the health and well-being of the people on your caseload. Most importantly, though, is the ability to be caring and compassionate, and to keep your focus where it belongs: people first. It's easy to get caught up in the stress of managing the business aspect of it all, making sure state or federal requirements are being met, that required paperwork is in order and meets their standards—but you have to remember that it's really about the people: first and foremost, the individuals on your caseload.

Q. **What advice would you give to high school students who are interested in this career?**

A. I don't think there is a lot of coursework to recommend at the high school level: perhaps psychology classes, if they are available. It's probably best to focus on the course work that will get you admitted to the college or university of your choice. If your high school has a special education student population, check to see if there is a mentoring program—some schools will match you with a student with special needs. You can also volunteer with organizations like the Special Olympics and community outreach organizations to gain exposure to the different types of populations you might serve as a case manager.

Interpreters and Translators

QUICK FACTS

School Subjects
English
Foreign language
Speech

Personal Skills
Communication/ideas
Helping/teaching

Work Environment
Primarily indoors
Primarily multiple locations

Minimum Education Level
Bachelor's degree

Salary Range
$25,623 to $47,690 to
$100,000

Certification or Licensing
Recommended

Outlook
Faster than the average

DOT
137

GOE
01.03.01

NOC
5125

O*NET-SOC
27-3091.00

OVERVIEW

An *interpreter* translates spoken passages of a foreign language into another specified language. The job is often designated by the language interpreted, such as Spanish or Japanese. In addition, many interpreters specialize according to subject matter. For example, *medical interpreters* have extensive knowledge of and experience in the health care field, while *court* or *judiciary interpreters* speak both a second language and the "language" of law. *Interpreters for the deaf*, also known as *sign language interpreters*, aid in the communication between people who are unable to hear and those who can.

In contrast to interpreters, *translators* focus on written materials, such as books, plays, technical or scientific papers, legal documents, laws, treaties, and decrees. A *sight translator* performs a combination of interpreting and translating by reading printed material in one language while reciting it aloud in another.

There are approximately 31,000 interpreters and translators employed in the United States.

HISTORY

Until recently, most people who spoke two languages well enough to interpret and translate did so only on the side, working full time in some other occupation. For example, many diplomats and high-level government officials employed people who were able to serve as interpreters and translators, but only as needed. These employees spent the rest of their time assisting in other ways.

Interpreting and translating as full-time professions have emerged only recently, partly in response to the need for high-speed communication across the globe. The increasing use of complex diplomacy has also increased demand for full-time translating and interpreting professionals. For many years, diplomacy was practiced largely between just two nations. Rarely did conferences involve more than two languages at one time. The League of Nations, established by the Treaty of Versailles in 1919, established a new pattern of communication. Although the language of diplomacy was then considered to be French, diplomatic discussions were carried out in many different languages for the first time.

Since the early 1920s, multinational conferences have become commonplace. Trade and educational conferences are now held with participants of many nations in attendance. Responsible for international diplomacy after the League of Nations dissolved, the United Nations (UN) now employs many full-time interpreters and translators, providing career opportunities for qualified people. In addition, the European Union employs a large number of interpreters.

In addition to employment with the United Nations and governmental agencies, interpreters and translators are now finding opportunities in legal, medical, business, and educational settings.

THE JOB

Although interpreters are needed for a variety of languages and different venues and circumstances, there are only two basic systems of interpretation: simultaneous and consecutive. Spurred in part by the invention and development of electronic sound equipment, simultaneous interpretation has been in use since the charter of the UN.

Simultaneous interpreters are able to convert a spoken sentence instantaneously. Some are so skilled that they are able to complete a sentence in the second language at almost the precise moment that the speaker is conversing in the original language. Such interpreters are usually familiar with the speaking habits of the speaker and can anticipate the way in which the sentence will be completed. The interpreter may also make judgments about the intent of the sentence or phrase from the speaker's gestures, facial expressions, and inflections. While working at a fast pace, the interpreter must be careful not to summarize, edit, or in any way change the meaning of what is being said.

In contrast, *consecutive interpreters* wait until the speaker has paused to convert speech into a second language. In this case, the speaker waits until the interpreter has finished before resuming the speech. Since every sentence is repeated in consecutive interpretation, this method takes longer than simultaneous interpretation.

In both systems, interpreters are placed so that they can clearly see and hear all that is taking place. In formal situations, such as those at the UN and other international conferences, interpreters are often assigned to a glass-enclosed booth. Speeches are transmitted to the booth, and interpreters, in turn, translate the speaker's words into a microphone. Each UN delegate can tune in the voice of the appropriate interpreter. Because of the difficulty of the job, these simultaneous interpreters usually work in pairs, each working 30-minute shifts.

All international *conference interpreters* are simultaneous interpreters. Many interpreters, however, work in situations other than formal diplomatic meetings. For example, interpreters are needed for negotiations of all kinds, as well as for legal, financial, medical, educational, and business purposes. Court or judiciary interpreters, for example, work in courtrooms and at attorney-client meetings, depositions, and witness preparation sessions. Medical interpreters are employed by for-profit and nonprofit hospitals, clinics, and other health care organizations to help medical professionals communicate with patients who do not speak English. Some interpreters may work for international humanitarian organizations such as the Red Cross. When a tsunami destroyed coastal communities across southern and Southeast Asia in 2004, interpreters who were proficient in Sinhala, Tamil, Hindi, and other languages were sent to the area to help with relief efforts.

Interpreters also work on short-term assignments. Services may be required for only brief intervals, such as for a special conference, a single interview with press representatives, or to translate for a single patient from Nepal who was brought to a hospital emergency room with chest pains.

While interpreters focus on the spoken word, translators work with written language. They read and translate novels, plays, essays, nonfiction and technical works, legal documents, records and reports, speeches, and other written material. Translators generally follow a certain set of procedures in their work. They begin by reading the text, taking careful notes on what they do not understand. To translate questionable passages, they look up words and terms in specialized dictionaries and glossaries. They may also do additional reading on the subject to arrive at a better understanding. Finally, they write translated drafts in the target language.

Localization translation is a relatively new specialty. *Localization translators* adapt computer software, Web sites, and other business products for use in a different language or culture.

REQUIREMENTS

High School

If you are interested in becoming an interpreter or translator, you should take a variety of English courses, because most translating work is from a foreign language into English. The study of one or more foreign languages is vital. If you are interested in becoming proficient in one or more of the Romance languages, such as Italian, French, or Spanish, basic courses in Latin will be valuable.

While you should devote as much time as possible to the study of at least one foreign language, other helpful courses include speech, business, cultural studies, humanities, world history, geography, and political science. In fact, any course that emphasizes the written and/or spoken word will be valuable to aspiring interpreters or translators. In addition, knowledge of a particular subject matter in which you may have interest, such as health, law, or science, will give you a professional edge if you want to specialize. Finally, courses in typing and word processing are recommended, especially if you want to pursue a career as a translator.

Postsecondary Training

Because interpreters and translators need to be proficient in grammar, have an excellent vocabulary in the chosen language, and have sound knowledge in a wide variety of subjects, employers generally require that applicants have at least a bachelor's degree. Scientific and professional interpreters are best qualified if they have graduate degrees.

In addition to language and field-specialty skills, you should take college courses that will allow you to develop effective techniques in public speaking, particularly if you're planning to pursue a career as an interpreter. Courses such as speech and debate will improve your diction and confidence as a public speaker.

Hundreds of colleges and universities in the United States offer degrees in languages. In addition, educational institutions now provide programs and degrees specialized for interpreting and translating. Georgetown University (http://linguistics.georgetown.edu/) offers both undergraduate and graduate programs in linguistics. Graduate degrees in interpretation and translation may be earned at the University of California at Santa Barbara (http://www.ucsb.edu), the University of Puerto Rico (http://www.upr.clu.edu), and the Monterey Institute of International Studies (http://www.miis.edu/languages.html). Many of these programs include both general and specialized courses, such as medical interpretation and legal translation.

Academic programs for the training of interpreters can be found in Europe as well. The University of Geneva's School of Translation and Interpretation (http://www.unige.ch/en) is highly regarded among professionals in the field.

Certification or Licensing

Although interpreters and translators need not be certified to obtain jobs, employers often show preference to certified applicants. Certification in Spanish, Haitian Creole, and Navajo is also required for interpreters who are employed by federal courts. State and local courts often have their own specific certification requirements. The National Center for State Courts has more information on certification for these workers. Interpreters for the deaf who pass an examination may qualify for either comprehensive or legal certification by the Registry of Interpreters for the Deaf. The U.S. Department of State has a three-test requirement for interpreters. These include simple consecutive interpreting (escort), simultaneous interpreting (court/seminar), and conference-level interpreting (international conferences). Applicants must have several years of foreign language practice, advanced education in the language (preferably abroad), and be fluent in vocabulary for a very broad range of subjects.

Foreign language translators may be granted certification by the American Translators Association (ATA) upon successful completion of required exams. ATA certification is available for translators who translate the following languages into English: Arabic, Croatian, Danish, Dutch, French, German, Hungarian, Japanese, Polish, Portuguese, Russian, and Spanish. Certification is also available for translators who translate English into the following languages: Chinese, Croatian, Dutch, Finnish, French, German, Hungarian, Italian, Japanese, Polish, Portuguese, Russian, Spanish, and Ukrainian.

Other Requirements

Interpreters should be able to speak at least two languages fluently, without strong accents. They should be knowledgeable of not only the foreign language but also of the culture and social norms of the region or country in which it is spoken. Both interpreters and translators should read daily newspapers in the languages in which they work to keep current in both developments and usage.

Interpreters must have good hearing, a sharp mind, and a strong, clear, and pleasant voice. They must be able to be precise and quick in their translation. In addition to being flexible and versatile in their work, both interpreters and translators should have self-discipline and patience. Above all, they should have an interest in and love of language.

An interpreter translates for a manager of refugee services at the Mohawk Valley Refugee Center in Utica, New York. The manager is explaining services to Somali refugees who have recently immigrated to the United States. *(Peter Chen, Syracuse Newspapers, The Image Works)*

Finally, interpreters must be honest and trustworthy, observing any existing codes of confidentiality at all times. The ethical code of interpreters and translators is a rigid one. They must hold private proceedings in strict confidence. Ethics also demands that interpreters and translators not distort the meaning of the sentences that are spoken or written. No matter how much they may agree or disagree with the speaker or writer, interpreters and translators must be objective in their work. In addition, information they obtain in the process of interpretation or translation must never be passed along to unauthorized people or groups.

EXPLORING

If you have an opportunity to visit the United Nations, you can watch the proceedings to get some idea of the techniques and responsibilities of the job of the interpreter. Occasionally, an international conference session is televised, and the work of the interpreters can be observed. You should note, however, that interpreters who work at these conferences are in the top positions of the vocation. Not everyone may aspire to such jobs. The work of interpreters and translators is usually less public, but not necessarily less interesting. If you are interested in interpreting or translating careers in health care, law, education, or other areas, ask your foreign language teacher to arrange an information interview with a worker in one of these settings.

If you have adequate skills in a foreign language, you might consider traveling in a country in which the language is spoken. If you can converse easily and without a strong accent and can interpret to others who may not understand the language well, you may have what it takes to work as an interpreter or translator.

For any international field, it is important that you familiarize yourself with other cultures. You can even arrange to regularly correspond with a pen pal in a foreign country. You may also want to join a school club that focuses on a particular language, such as the French Club or the Spanish Club. If no such clubs exist, consider forming one. Student clubs can allow you to hone your foreign language speaking and writing skills and learn about other cultures.

Finally, participating on a speech or debate team can allow you to practice your public speaking skills, increase your confidence, and polish your overall appearance by working on eye contact, gestures, facial expressions, tone, and other elements used in public speaking.

EMPLOYERS

There are approximately 31,000 interpreters and translators in the United States. Although many interpreters and translators work for government or international agencies, some are employed by private firms. Large import-export companies often have interpreters or translators on their payrolls, although these employees generally perform additional duties for the firm. International banks, companies, organizations, and associations often employ both interpreters and translators to facilitate communication. In addition, translators and interpreters work at nonprofit organizations, publishing houses, schools, bilingual newspapers, radio and television stations, airlines, shipping companies, law firms, and scientific and medical operations.

While translators are employed nationwide, a large number of interpreters find work in New York and Washington, D.C. Among the largest employers of interpreters and translators are the United Nations, the World Bank, the U.S. Department of State, the Bureau of the Census, the CIA, the FBI, the Library of Congress, the Red Cross, the YMCA, and the armed forces.

Finally, many interpreters and translators work independently in private practice. These self-employed professionals must be disciplined and driven, since they must handle all aspects of the business such as scheduling work and billing clients.

STARTING OUT

Most interpreters and translators begin as part-time freelancers until they gain experience and contacts in the field. Individuals can apply for jobs directly to the hiring firm, agency, or organization. Many of these employers advertise available positions in the classified section of the newspaper or on the Internet. In addition, contact your college career services office and language department to inquire about job leads.

While many opportunities exist, top interpreting and translating jobs are hard to obtain since the competition for these higher profile positions is fierce. You may be wise to develop supplemental skills that can be attractive to employers while refining your interpreting and translating techniques. The UN, for example, employs administrative assistants who can take shorthand and transcribe notes in two or more languages. The UN also hires tour guides who speak more than one language. Such positions can be initial steps toward your future career goals.

ADVANCEMENT

Competency in language determines the speed of advancement for interpreters and translators. Job opportunities and promotions are plentiful for those who have acquired great proficiency in languages. However, interpreters and translators need to constantly work and study to keep abreast of the changing linguistic trends for a given language. The constant addition of new vocabulary for technological advances, inventions, and processes keep languages fluid. Those who do not keep up with changes will find that their communication skills become quickly outdated.

Interpreters and translators who work for government agencies advance by clearly defined grade promotions. Those who work for other organizations can aspire to become chief interpreters or chief translators, or reviewers who check the work of others.

Although advancement in the field is generally slow, interpreters and translators will find many opportunities to succeed as freelancers. Some can even establish their own bureaus or agencies.

EARNINGS

Earnings for interpreters and translators vary depending on experience, skills, number of languages used, and employers. In government, trainee interpreters and translators generally begin at the GS-5 rating, earning from $25,623 to $33,309 a year in 2007. Those with a college degree can start at the higher GS-7 level, earning from

$31,740 to $41,262. With an advanced degree, trainees begin at the GS-9 ($38,824 to $50,470), GS-10 ($42,755 to $55,580), or GS-11 level ($46,974 to $61,068).

Interpreters who are employed by the United Nations work under a salary structure called the Common System. In 2007, UN short-term interpreters (workers employed for a duration of 60 days or less) had daily gross pay of $492.50 (Grade I) or $321.50 (Grade II). UN short-term translators and revisers had daily gross pay of $192.85 (Translator I), $236.95 (Translator II), $280.85 (Translator III/Reviser I), $316.35 (Translator IV/Reviser II), or $351.85 (Reviser III).

The U.S. Department of Labor reports the following mean annual salaries for interpreters and translators by specialty in 2006: junior colleges, $45,800; general medical and surgical hospitals, $38,340; local government, $35,200; and elementary and secondary schools, $33,680.

Interpreters employed by nonprofit organizations had median annual incomes of $47,690 in 2006, according to *Compensation in Nonprofit Organizations 2006*, a report from Abbott, Langer & Associates.

Interpreters and translators who work on a freelance basis usually charge by the word, the page, the hour, or the project. Freelance interpreters for international conferences or meetings can earn between $300 and $500 a day from the U.S. government. By the hour, freelance translators usually earn between $15 and $35; however, rates vary depending on the language and the subject matter. Book translators work under contract with publishers. These contracts cover the fees that are to be paid for translating work as well as royalties, advances, penalties for late payments, and other provisions.

Interpreters and translators working in a specialized field have high earning potential. According to the National Association of Judiciary Interpreters and Translators, the federal courts pay $305 per day for court interpreters. Most work as freelancers, earning annual salaries from $30,000 to $100,000 a year.

Interpreters who work for the deaf also may work on a freelance basis, earning anywhere from $12 to $40 an hour, according to the Registry of Interpreters for the Deaf. Those employed with an agency, government organization, or school system can earn up to $30,000 to start; in urban areas, $40,000 to $50,000 a year.

Depending on the employer, interpreters and translators often enjoy such benefits as health and life insurance, pension plans, and paid vacation and sick days.

WORK ENVIRONMENT

Interpreters and translators work under a wide variety of circumstances and conditions. As a result, most do not have typical nine-to-five schedules.

Conference interpreters probably have the most comfortable physical facilities in which to work. Their glass-enclosed booths are well lit and temperature controlled. Court or judiciary interpreters work in courtrooms or conference rooms, while interpreters for the deaf work at educational institutions as well as a wide variety of other locations. Medical interpreters work in emergency rooms, offices of physicians, and other health care settings. Interpreters who are employed by the Red Cross and other humanitarian organizations often work in dangerous settings such as war zones and areas that have been affected by natural disasters such as floods, tornados, earthquakes, and hurricanes.

Translators usually work in offices, although many spend considerable time in libraries and research centers. Freelance translators often work at home, using their own personal computers, the Internet, dictionaries, and other resource materials.

While both interpreting and translating require flexibility and versatility, interpreters in particular, especially those who work for international congresses or courts or humanitarian organizations, may experience considerable stress and fatigue. Knowing that a great deal depends upon their absolute accuracy in interpretation can be a weighty responsibility.

OUTLOOK

Employment opportunities for interpreters and translators are expected to grow faster than the average for all occupations through 2014, according to the U.S. Department of Labor. However, competition for available positions will be fierce. With the explosion of such technologies as the Internet, lightning-fast Internet connections, and videoconferencing, global communication has taken great strides. In short, the world has become smaller, so to speak, creating a demand for professionals to aid in the communication between people of different languages and cultural backgrounds.

In addition to new technological advances, demographic factors will fuel demand for translators and interpreters. Although some immigrants who come to the United States assimilate easily with respect to culture and language, many have difficulty learning English. As immigration to the United States continues to increase, interpreters and translators will be needed to help immigrants function in an English-speaking society. According to Ann Macfarlane, past president of the American Translators Association, "community interpreting" for immigrants and refugees is a challenging area requiring qualified language professionals.

Another demographic factor influencing the interpreting and translating fields is the growth in overseas travel. Americans on average are spending an increasing amount of money on travel, especially to foreign countries. The resulting growth of the travel industry will create a need for interpreters to lead tours, both at home and abroad.

In addition to leisure travel, business travel is spurring the need for more translators and interpreters. With workers traveling abroad in growing numbers to attend meetings, conferences, and seminars with overseas clients, interpreters and translators will be needed to help bridge both the language and cultural gaps.

While no more than a few thousand interpreters and translators are employed in the largest markets (the federal government and international organizations), other job options exist. The medical field, for example, will provide many jobs for language professionals, translating such products as pharmaceutical inserts, research papers, and medical reports for insurance companies. Interpreters will also be needed to provide non-English speakers with language assistance in health care settings. Opportunities exist for qualified individuals in law, trade and business, health care, tourism, recreation, and the government.

The U.S. Department of Labor predicts that employment growth will be limited for conference interpreters and literary translators.

FOR MORE INFORMATION

For information on careers in literary translation, contact
American Literary Translators Association
University of Texas-Dallas
Box 830688, Mail Station JO51
Richardson, TX 75083-0688
http://www.utdallas.edu/alta

For more on the translating and interpreting professions, including information on certification, contact
American Translators Association
225 Reinekers Lane, Suite 590
Alexandria, VA 22314-2875
Tel: 703-683-6100
Email: ata@atanet.org
http://www.atanet.org

For information on employment in the nonprofit sector, contact the following organizations:

Council on Foundations
1828 L Street, NW, Suite 300
Washington, DC 20036-5104
Tel: 202-466-6512
Email: info@cof.org
http://www.cof.org

Foundation Center
79 Fifth Avenue & 16th Street
New York, NY 10003-3076
Tel: 800-424-9836
http://foundationcenter.org

National Council of Nonprofit Associations
1101 Vermont Avenue, NW, Suite 1002
Washington, DC 20005-3560
Tel: 202-962-0322
http://www.ncna.org

For more information on court interpreting and certification, contact
National Association of Judiciary Interpreters and Translators
1707 L Street, NW, Suite 507
Washington, DC 20036-4201
Tel: 202-293-0342
Email: headquarters@najit.org
http://www.najit.org

For information on interpreter training programs for working with the deaf and certification, contact
Registry of Interpreters for the Deaf
333 Commerce Street
Alexandria, VA 22314-2801
Tel: 703-838-0030
http://www.rid.org

For information on union membership for freelance interpreters and translators, contact
Translators and Interpreters Guild
962 Wayne Avenue, Suite 500
Silver Spring, MD 20910-4432
Tel: 800-992-0367

Investment Professionals

QUICK FACTS

School Subjects
Business
Mathematics

Personal Skills
Communication/ideas
Leadership/management

Work Environment
Primarily indoors
Primarily one location

Minimum Education Level
Bachelor's degree

Salary Range
$40,340 to $66,590 to
$130,130+

Certification or Licensing
Recommended (certification)
Required for certain
positions (licensing)

Outlook
Faster than the average

DOT
N/A

GOE
N/A

NOC
1112

O*NET-SOC
13-2051.00

OVERVIEW

Foundations rely on a team of professionals to manage their funds. *Investment professionals* such as *financial analysts, fund managers, endowment managers,* and *chief investment officers* are responsible for creating an investment strategy to keep the foundation's initial endowment intact, but also to increase its assets. They often rely on a staff of accountants and consultants for help with various projects.

HISTORY

Ever since the first philanthropic organizations were founded, investment professionals were needed to help manage and grow their endowments, as well as help manage any other funds that were donated to the organization. The amount and financial health of its holdings guaranteed the continued existence of the foundation and its grant-making capacities. Today, investment professionals are integral members of a foundation's management team, overseeing endowments that range from hundreds of thousands of dollars to more than $1 billion.

THE JOB

Investment professionals work in many industries, but their role in the nonprofit sector is quite different from that with for-profit organizations. Most private foundations have an initial donation or endowment from which to disperse grants and loans (typically, 5 percent of the endowment is used each year for grants and loans). It is important for the future of the foundation to keep this initial sum replenished through investments, or better yet, find investments to increase the assets of the foundation.

Investment professionals study their employer's financial status and make financial and investment recommendations. To arrive at these recommendations, they examine their organization's financial history and objectives, income and expenditures, risk tolerance, and current investments. They identify the short- and long-term goals of the foundation. Are there new interests or projects the foundation wants to support through its philanthropy? Does it plan to renew its existing grants? Does it wish to work in partnership with other foundations to increase the power of its aid money?

Though the amount of investments will vary according to the size of the foundation and its holdings, most organizations channel their investments into a diversified portfolio. The Rockefeller Foundation, for example, has investments in numerous stock funds and bonds. A list of all foundation holdings is usually reported in a foundation's annual statement, or found on its Web site. Investment professionals closely monitor current investments, or active funds. They report details such as daily activity and interest, and post such information in the foundations' quarterly reports. They also receive and process any payments from these active investments.

They also deal with past investments, or inactive funds. Though such funds have closed, investment professionals still need to report on the fund's value and interest, and post this information in quarterly reports and on the foundation's Web site.

Other duties of investment professionals are administrative in nature. Beside compiling quarterly and annual financial reports, they may be responsible for a grant's payout schedule, establishing financial procedures, keeping financial records for operating and administrative expenses, and hiring and training investment department staff members.

Smaller foundations may not have the financial means to staff its own investment team, but rather outsource this position. Many accounting and financial consulting firms specialize in serving nonprofit organizations.

REQUIREMENTS

High School

Since investment professionals work with numbers and compile data, you should take as many math classes as you can. Accounting, business, economics, and computer classes will be helpful as well. A good grasp of computer spreadsheet programs such as Excel is vital. Take extra care as you research and write reports in any subject matter or in public speaking, and it will pay off later when you must conduct investment research and write and present investment recommendations.

Postsecondary Training

Most employers require that investment professionals hold a bachelor's degree in accounting, business administration, finance, or statistics. Other possible majors include communications, economics, international business, and public administration. Some organizations will hire you if you hold a bachelor's degree in another discipline as long as you can demonstrate mathematical ability. In college, take business, economics, and statistics courses. Since computer technology plays such a big role in this work, computer classes can be helpful as well. English composition classes can prepare you for the writing you will need to do when preparing reports. Some employers require a writing sample prior to an interview.

Some colleges and universities offer financial classes tailored to those wishing to work in the nonprofit sector.

Certification or Licensing

Financial analysts can earn the title chartered financial analyst (CFA). While certification is not required, it is recommended. The CFA program, which is administered by the CFA Institute, consists of three levels of examinations. These rigorous exams deal with such topics as economics, financial statement analysis, and portfolio management. While not specifically geared toward investment professionals who are employed in the nonprofit sector, the certification is recognized around the world as a standard in the finance industry.

For certain upper-level positions, some organizations may require that you have a certified public accountant license.

Other Requirements

Beside investment savvy, the most successful investment professionals have excellent leadership and organizational skills, as well as a keen eye for detail. They are also able to be firm, yet tactful, when dealing with foundation board members and other departmental directors. Investment professionals should be able to clearly communicate ideas, both verbally when making presentations and on paper when writing reports.

EXPLORING

There are many sources of information dealing with the financial services industry. Read publications such as *Barron's* (http://www. barrons.com), *Wall Street Journal* (http://www.wsj.com), *Forbes* (http://www.forbes.com), *BusinessWeek* (http://www.business week.com), *Fortune* (http://www.fortune.com), and *Financial Times* (http://www.ft.com). In the print or online versions, you will find a wealth of information on stocks, mutual funds, finance, education, careers, salaries, global business, and more. You can also conduct company research. You might have to become a subscriber to access certain sections online.

While in high school, you might volunteer to handle the book-keeping for a school club or student government, or help balance the family checking account to become familiar with simple book-keeping practices. Your school may have an investment club you can join. If not, ask a parent or teacher to help you research and analyze investment opportunities. Choose a specific industry (e.g., telecommunications, technology, or health care), study companies in that industry, and select and track several stocks that appear to have growth potential.

EMPLOYERS

Foundations are located throughout the United States, yet the best employment prospects are located within the "foundation cluster" region—New York's metropolitan area, Los Angeles, Chicago, Washington, D.C., and the San Francisco Bay area. Many of the nation's largest foundations are located in these metropolitan areas.

Investment professionals not employed by nonprofit organizations can still work in the industry as consultants. Many accounting firms offer investment consulting on a project basis, or may work on a retainer. This is especially helpful for smaller foundations that may not have the means to staff a full-time financial department.

STARTING OUT

Working as a fund manager or analyst may be a great way to break into the world of nonprofit investment but these positions are in no way considered entry level. Such jobs are usually awarded to individuals with at least a bachelor's degree or prior work experience in the field of finance.

Other professionals transfer to the nonprofit sector after long, successful careers in the for-profit sector. Many identify with the missions and goals of foundations, and are interested in helping a particular cause.

ADVANCEMENT

With advanced education and work experience, lower-level investment professionals, such as accountants and analysts, can hope for promotions to the position of fund manager, endowment manager, or director of finance. Investment professionals may face stiff competition for top positions—chief investment officer, for example. Executive jobs are scarce since only the largest of foundations would need, or have the means, for such positions.

Many talented individuals transfer from private foundations to community foundations. Others may choose to be active in other nonprofit departments such as grant making or public relations.

EARNINGS

There is no salary information available for investment professionals employed by nonprofit organizations. The U.S. Department of Labor reports that median annual earnings of financial analysts employed in all industries were $66,590 in 2006. Top earners (the top 10 percent) made more than $130,130, and the lowest salaries (the lowest 10 percent) were less than $40,340. Benefits include paid vacation, health, disability, life insurance, and retirement or pension plans.

WORK ENVIRONMENT

Most investment professionals work in an office setting. Some may work out of their homes. They spend much of their time working on a computer, doing research, and compiling data. If employed full time, they typically work a standard 40-hour week.

OUTLOOK

Foundations will always need trained professionals to manage their endowments and other funds. Opportunities will be best at large foundations, which are often located in large cities. Overall, the U.S. Department of Labor predicts that employment for financial analysts (a subcategory of investment professionals) employed in all industries will grow faster than the average for all occupations through 2014.

FOR MORE INFORMATION

For a helpful dictionary of financial terminology, visit the association's Web site:

Association for Financial Professionals
4520 East West Highway, Suite 750
Bethesda, MD 20814-3574
Tel: 301-907-2862
http://www.afponline.org

For information on certification, contact

CFA Institute
560 Ray C. Hunt Drive
Charlottesville, VA 22903-2981
Tel: 800-247-8132
Email: info@cfainstitute.org
http://www.cfainstitute.org

For information on careers with foundations, contact

Foundation Financial Officers Group
Email: info@ffog.org
http://ffog.org/account/activities

Lobbyists

QUICK FACTS

School Subjects
Government
Journalism
Speech

Personal Skills
Communication/ideas
Leadership/management

Work Environment
Primarily indoors
One location with some
    travel

Minimum Education Level
Bachelor's degree

Salary Range
$20,000 to $86,000 to
    $500,000+

Certification or Licensing
None available

Outlook
About as fast as the average

DOT
165

GOE
N/A

NOC
N/A

O*NET-SOC
N/A

OVERVIEW

A *lobbyist* works to influence legislation on the federal, state, or local level on behalf of clients. Nonprofit organizations, labor unions, trade associations, corporations, and other groups and individuals use lobbyists to voice concerns and opinions to government representatives. Lobbyists use their knowledge of the legislative process and their government contacts to represent their clients' interests. Though most lobbyists are based in Washington, D.C., many work throughout the country representing client issues in city and state government.

HISTORY

Lobbying has been a practice within government since colonial times. In the late 1700s, the term *lobbyist* was used to describe the special-interest representatives who gathered in the anteroom outside the legislative chamber in the New York state capitol. The term often had a negative connotation, with political cartoonists frequently portraying lobbyists as slick, cigar-chomping individuals attempting to buy favors. But in the 20th century, lobbyists came to be looked upon as experts in the fields that they represented, and members of Congress relied upon them to provide information needed to evaluate legislation. During the New Deal in the 1930s, government spending in Washington greatly increased, and the number of lobbyists proliferated proportionately. A major lobbying law was enacted in 1938, but it was not until 1946 that comprehensive legislation in the form of the Federal Regulation of Lobbying Act was passed into law. The act requires that anyone who spends or receives money or anything of value in the interests of passing, modifying, or defeating legislation being considered by the U.S. Congress be registered and provide spending reports. Its effectiveness, however, was reduced by vague language that frequently required legal interpretations. Further regulatory acts have been passed in the years since; most recently, the Lobbying Disclosure Act of 1995 has required registration of all lobbyists working at the federal level.

THE JOB

An example of effective lobbying concerns MedicAlert, an organization that provides bracelets to millions of people in the United States and Canada with health problems. Engraved on the bracelet is a description of the person's medical problem, along with MedicAlert's 24-hour emergency response phone number. The emergency response center is located in a region of California that considered changing the telephone area code. MedicAlert anticipated a lot of confusion—and many possible medical disasters—if the area code was changed from that which is engraved on the millions of bracelets. MedicAlert called upon doctors, nurses, and the media to get word out about the danger to lives. Through this lobbying, the public and the state's policy makers became aware of an important aspect of the area code change they may not have otherwise known.

The MedicAlert Foundation, like the thousands of associations, unions, and corporations in the United States, benefited from using lobbyists with an understanding of state politics and influence. The ASAE/Center for Association Leadership estimates that the number of national trade and charitable associations exceeds 20,000. With 3,500 of these associations based in Washington, D.C., associations are the third-largest industry in the city, behind government and tourism. Lobbyists may work for one of these associations as a director of government relations, or they may work for an industry, company, or other organization to act on its behalf in government concerns. Lobbyists also work for lobbying firms that work with many different clients on a contractual basis.

Lobbyists have years of experience working with the government, learning about federal and state politics, and meeting career politicians and their staffs. Their job is to make members of Congress aware of the issues of concern to their clients and the effect that legislation and regulations will have on them. They provide the members of Congress with research and analysis to help them make the most informed decisions possible. Lobbyists also keep their clients informed with updates and reports.

Lobbying techniques are generally broken down into two broad categories: direct lobbying and indirect, or "grassroots," lobbying. Direct lobbying techniques include making personal contacts with members of Congress and appointed officials. It is important for lobbyists to know who the key people are in drafting legislation that is significant to their clientele. They hire technical experts to develop reports, charts, graphs, or schematic drawings that may help in the legislative decision-making process that determines the passage, amendment, or defeat of a measure. Sometimes a lobbyist with expertise on a particular issue works directly with a member of Congress in the drafting of a bill. Lobbyists also keep members of Congress tuned in to the voices of their constituents.

Indirect, or grassroots, lobbying involves persuading voters to support a client's view. If the member of Congress knows that a majority of voters favor a particular point of view, he or she will support or fight legislation according to the voters' wishes. Probably the most widely used method of indirect lobbying is the letter-writing campaign. Lobbyists use direct mail, newsletters, media advertising, and other methods of communication to reach constituents and convince them to write to their member of Congress with their supporting views. Lobbyists also use phone campaigns, encouraging the constituents to call their Congress member's office. Aides usually tally the calls that come in and communicate the volume to the legislator.

Indirect lobbying is also done through the media. Lobbyists try to persuade newspaper and magazine editors and radio and television news managers to write or air editorials that reflect the point of view of their clientele. They write op-ed pieces that are submitted to the media for publication. They arrange for experts to speak in favor of a particular position on talk shows or to make statements that are picked up by the media. As a persuasive measure, lobbyists may send a legislator a collection of news clippings indicating public opinion on a forthcoming measure, or provide tapes of aired editorials and news features covering a relevant subject.

REQUIREMENTS

High School

Becoming a lobbyist requires years of experience in other government and related positions. To prepare for a government job, take courses in history, social studies, and civics to learn about the structure of local, state, and federal government. English and composition classes will help you develop your communication skills. Work on the student council or become an officer for a school club. Taking journalism courses and working on the school newspaper will prepare you for the public relations aspect of lobbying. As a reporter you will research current issues, meet with policy makers, and write articles.

Postsecondary Training

As a rule, people take up lobbying after having left an earlier career. Some lobbyists have worked as appointed or elected officials or congressional staff members; others have backgrounds in private industry. Schools do not generally offer a specific curriculum that leads to a career as a lobbyist; your experience with legislation and policymaking is what will prove valuable to employers and clients. Almost all lobbyists have college degrees, and many have graduate degrees. Degrees in law and political science are among the most beneficial for prospective lobbyists, just as they are for other careers in politics and government. Journalism, education, public relations, history, and economics are other areas of study that would be helpful in the pursuit of a lobbying career.

The American League of Lobbyists (ALL) offers a certificate program for newcomers to the field as well as experienced practitioners who are seeking to hone their skills. To complete the ALL Lobbying Certificate Program, applicants must take 11 of the following 15 sessions: Online Advocacy; Political Action Committees and Campaign Finance Rules & Regulations (required); Appropriations: Process and Implications; Lobbying Ethics (required); Drafting Legislation; Grassroots Lobbying and Coalition Building; Lobbying Disclosure Act and FARA Requirements (required); Communications: Effective Ways of Communicating with Congress, the Administration, Regulatory Agencies, and the Media; Budget: Process and Implications; Avoiding Conflicts of Interest; House & Senate Procedures (required); Lobbying the Executive Branch; House & Senate Rules (required); Government Contracting and the Regulatory Process; and The Lobbying Business: The Ins and Outs of Starting and Running a Lobbying Shop.

Certification or Licensing

Lobbyists do not need a license or certification, but are required to register. The Lobbying Disclosure Act of 1995 requires all lobbyists working on the federal level to register with the Secretary of the Senate and the Clerk of the House. You may also be required to register with the states in which you lobby and possibly pay a small fee.

There is no union available to lobbyists. Some lobbyists join the American League of Lobbyists, which provides a variety of support services for its members. Membership in a number of other

Lobbyists meet with lawmakers outside a government building in Texas. They need to have strong people skills to develop good relationships with legislators in order to serve their clients' interests. *(Bob Daemmrich, The Image Works)*

associations, including the ASAE/Center for Association Leadership and the American Association of Political Consultants, can also be useful to lobbyists.

Other Requirements

Lobbyists must have practical, everyday involvement in government and politics, as well as comprehensive knowledge of the issues for which they are lobbying.

Lobbyists should also be very honest since one's reputation is key to success in the field. You also need people skills to develop good relationships with legislators in order to serve your clients' interests. Your knowledge of the workings of government, along with good communication skills, will help you to explain government legislation to your clients in ways that they can clearly understand.

EXPLORING

To explore this career, become an intern or volunteer in the office of a lobbyist, legislator, government official, special interest group, or nonprofit institution (especially one that relies on government grants). Working in these fields will introduce you to the lobbyist's world and provide early exposure to the workings of government.

Another good way to learn more about this line of work is by becoming involved in your school government; writing for your school newspaper; doing public relations, publicity, and advertising work for school and community organizations; and taking part in fund-raising drives. When major legislative issues are being hotly debated, you can write to your congressional representatives to express your views or even organize a letter writing or telephone campaign; these actions are in themselves forms of lobbying.

EMPLOYERS

Organizations either hire government liaisons to handle lobbying or they contract with law and lobby firms. Liaisons who work for one organization work on only those issues that affect that organization. Independent lobbyists work on a variety of different issues, taking on clients on a contractual basis. They may contract with large corporations, such as a pharmaceutical or communications company, as well as volunteer services to nonprofit organizations. Lobbying firms are located all across the country. Those executives in charge of government relations for trade associations and other organizations are generally based in Washington, D.C.

STARTING OUT

Lobbyist positions will not be listed in the classifieds. It takes years of experience and an impressive list of connections to find a government relations job in an organization. Professional lobbyists usually have backgrounds as lawyers, public relations executives, congressional aides, legislators, government officials, or professionals in business and industry. Once established in a government or law career, lobbyists begin to hear about corporations and associations that need knowledgeable people for their government relations departments. The ASAE/Center for Association Leadership hosts a Web site, http://www.asaenet.org, which lists available positions for executives with trade associations.

ADVANCEMENT

Lobbyists focus on developing long-standing relationships with legislators and clients and become experts on policymaking and legislation. Association or company executives may advance from a position as director of government relations into a position as president or vice-president. Lobbyists who contract their services to various clients advance by taking on more clients and working for larger corporations.

EARNINGS

Because of the wide range of salaries earned by lobbyists, it is difficult to compile an accurate survey. Abbott, Langer & Associates, however, regularly conducts surveys of association executives. According to *Compensation in Nonprofit Organizations 2006*, a report from the organization, directors of government relations had median annual incomes of $86,000 in 2006. Compensation varies greatly depending on location, with directors employed in large cities—especially New York, Washington, D.C., and Chicago—earning more than those employed in smaller cities.

Like lawyers, lobbyists are considered very well paid; also like lawyers, a lobbyist's income depends on the size of the organization he or she represents. Experienced contract lobbyists with a solid client base can earn well over $100,000 a year and some make more than $500,000 a year. Beginning lobbyists may make less than $20,000 a year as they build a client base. In many cases, a lobbyist may take on large corporations as clients for the bulk of the annual income, then volunteer services to nonprofit organizations.

WORK ENVIRONMENT

Lobbyists spend much of their time communicating with the people who affect legislation—principally the legislators and officials of federal and state governments. This communication takes place in person, by telephone, and by memoranda. Most of a lobbyist's time is spent gathering information, writing reports, creating publicity, and staying in touch with clients. They respond to the public and the news media when required. Sometimes their expertise is required at hearings or they may testify before a legislature.

OUTLOOK

The number of special interest groups in the United States continues to grow, and as long as they continue to plead their causes before state and federal governments, lobbyists will be needed. However, lobbying cutbacks often occur in corporations. Because lobbying doesn't directly earn a profit for a business, the government relations department is often the first in a company to receive budget cuts. The American League of Lobbyists anticipates that the career will remain stable, though it's difficult to predict. In recent years, there has been a significant increase in registrations, but that is most likely a result of the Lobbying Disclosure Act of 1995 requiring registration.

The methods of grassroots advocacy will continue to be affected by the Internet and other new communication technology. Lobbyists and organizations use Web pages to inform the public of policy issues. These Web pages often include ways to immediately send e-mail messages to state and federal legislators. Constituents may have the choice of composing their own messages or sending messages already composed. With this method, a member of Congress can easily determine the feelings of the constituents based on the amount of email received.

FOR MORE INFORMATION

For information on membership, contact
American Association of Political Consultants
600 Pennsylvania Avenue, SE, Suite 330
Washington, DC 20003-6300
Tel: 202-544-9815
Email: info@theaapc.org
http://www.theaapc.org

For information about careers and its Lobbying Certificate Program, contact
American League of Lobbyists
PO Box 30005
Alexandria, VA 22310-8005
Tel: 703-960-3011
Email: alldc.org@erols.com
http://www.alldc.org

For information about government relations and public policy concerns within trade associations, contact
ASAE/Center for Association Leadership
1575 I Street, NW
Washington, DC 20005-1105
Tel: 888-950-2723
http://www.asaenet.org

Nonprofit Social Service Directors

QUICK FACTS

School Subjects
Government
Psychology
Sociology

Personal Skills
Helping/teaching
Leadership/management

Work Environment
Primarily indoors
Primarily one location

Minimum Education Level
Bachelor's degree

Salary Range
$56,500 to $100,118 to
$207,145+

Certification or Licensing
Required for certain positions

Outlook
Faster than the average

DOT
N/A

GOE
12.01.01

NOC
N/A

O*NET-SOC
11-9151.00

OVERVIEW

Nonprofit social service directors, also known as *nonprofit directors*, *nonprofit chief executive officers, nonprofit administrators*, or *social and community service managers*, are at the top rung on the agency's ladder. No matter what area the agency specializes in—health care, services for the aging, or youth development, for example—the director is the individual who spearheads the organization's efforts, operations, and progress. A director's duties may include hiring and managing staff, fund-raising, budgeting, public relations, and, depending on the agency, working directly with the clientele served.

HISTORY

Social service organizations have been around in various forms for hundreds of years. During the Middle Ages, organizations formed to care for the sick and the poor. By the 1800s, the industrial revolution was changing society's structure as numerous people moved from small towns and farms to cities where they worked in industries and had few, if any, established social support systems. The cities became more crowded, wages were low, and life became more complicated. After the Civil War, there was an explosion of social service organizations—groups caring for the sick and the poor, and, increasingly, for immigrants. Under President Roosevelt's administration during the 1930s, many New Deal programs, such as unemployment insurance, were established to help people deal with the effects of the Depression. During the 1960s, President Johnson's administration followed a similar agenda of promoting the well-being of all citizens with the "Great Society" programs, such as Medicare. These programs increased the role of the government in the welfare of individuals and stimulated the growth of private social service organizations. In the years that followed, the older organizations expanded and many new organizations emerged.

By the end of the 20th century, however, social support systems had begun to change. The federal government, responding to the unpopularity of the expense of many government social service programs, eliminated some programs and cut back on many others. Perhaps the best-known cutback was the Welfare Reform Bill, which was designed to shorten the length of time welfare recipients receive benefits. Reforms at the national level mean that state governments often find themselves trying to provide money to keep programs running. If the funds can't be found at the state level, the slack may be picked up at the city level. If the city is unable to come up with the necessary funds, the services usually pass out of the hands of governmental officials altogether and into the hands of local or national nonprofit organizations.

The need for nongovernmental organizations to fill in gaps left by federal, state, and local programs has changed the profile of charity work. Where many organizations once had untrained volunteers, they now often require trained, full-time staff. As nonprofit social service work has become more crucial to the national infrastructure, nonprofits have become increasingly professional. Nonprofit organizations are dependent on intelligent, educated, and savvy direction in order to work. Fund-raising, budgeting, resource management, and public relations are just a few areas where top-notch business skills are a necessity. The role of those who run the organizations—administrators, executive directors, and directors—is crucial.

THE JOB

Anyone looking for a career that provides a diversity of responsibilities, satisfaction, meaning, action, and a wide realm of options should certainly consider entering the field of social work. Social workers are people who are committed to making a positive difference in the human condition, and the director of an organization has the primary responsibility of seeing that the organization achieves its goals and impacts positively on the lives of the people it's designed to serve.

An aspect of social work that sets it apart from other helping professions is the concept of helping people in their environments. Social workers help clients not only with how they feel about a situation, but also with what they can do about it. For example, a woman suffering stress from being a single parent may be referred by a social worker to a child care agency. The social worker also might help her explore other options, such as getting flextime at work. In addition, the social worker might provide therapy or counseling or refer the client to a qualified therapist for assistance in managing her stress. A wide variety of nonprofit organizations are at work in the United States today, and each has a different mission and set of services.

Because it now takes such a high level of professional sophistication to keep a nonprofit going, directing these sorts of organizations is becoming a complex, challenging, and varied career. At one time, the biggest prerequisite to those who wanted to work in social services was a big heart. Today, compassion is still a necessary quality to have, but knowledge, skill, and talent are just as important. A director of a social services organization may be in charge of managing staff, overseeing the budget, spearheading fund-raising efforts, and handling public relations issues.

Sheri Flanigan served for three years as the executive director of La Casa Latina Inc., a nonprofit organization with the mission to "empower the Latino population to become part of the Siouxland community." Flanigan says about her work, "There was no 'typical day.' I spent about half of my time on administration: budgeting, fund-raising, grant writing, staff supervision, community meetings, and board meetings. Because we were small (five staff members and a $150,000 budget), I did all of the bookkeeping and payroll. The other half of my time, I provided direct services—translations and interpretation primarily. I also filled in when another staff member was out."

Flanigan notes that the diversity of her experiences was one of the best parts of the job. Because she worked for a small organization, she could work on both a macro and a micro level. She was able to see the fruits of her organization's labors on a community-wide level, but she also enjoyed the time she was able to spend working directly with the agency's clients.

In any nonprofit organization, even as the top individual in the structure, the nature of a director's work likely will be determined largely by a board of directors. This board, plus the size and nature of the organization, will define the director's duties to a large extent.

REQUIREMENTS

High School

If you're interested in nonprofit social services work, you'll want to concentrate on humanities and social science courses such as English, history, government, sociology, and psychology. Such courses will give you perspective on the issues confronting the people that a nonprofit organization will be trying to help. Communication skills are critical, so in addition to English, take public speaking courses to hone your skills. The ability to speak a foreign language will be a big plus in many organizations; consider taking Spanish, as it is the second most common language spoken in the United States. At the director level of a nonprofit agency, you will be responsible for budget expenditures; therefore, you should have mathematics and accounting knowledge, so be sure to include these classes in your schedule. Finally, take computer science courses so that you will be able to use the computer for activities such as creating budgets, writing grant proposals, and keeping a database of information on clients.

Postsecondary Training

Most nonprofit social service organizations will require that you have a degree in social work from a college or university program accredited by the Council on Social Work Education. The undergraduate degree is the bachelor of social work (BSW). Graduate degrees include the master of social work (MSW) and the doctorate in social work (DSW) or Ph.D. The undergraduate degree will allow you to find entry-level positions at many agencies. Typical courses of study for the BSW include classes in social welfare policies, human behavior and the social environment, research methods, and ethics. In addition, accredited programs require you to complete at least 400 hours of supervised field experience. To advance to the level of director, you will need to have a master's or doctorate degree. Obtaining an MSW degree usually requires two years of courses along with 900 hours of supervised fieldwork. You may be able to enter a master's program without having a BSW; however, you should have a background that includes psychology, sociology, biology, economics, and social work courses.

Certification or Licensing

According to the U.S. Department of Labor, all states have some type of licensing, certification, or registration requirement for those practicing social work and using professional titles. However, the standards and requirements vary from state to state, and those wanting to work as social workers will need to check with their state licensing boards. These licensing, certification, or registration requirements may or may not be necessary for the director, depending on the nature of the organization and the duties of the director. Again, those wanting to work as directors will need to contact the regulatory board of the state in which they want to work to find out specific requirements. The Association of Social Work Boards may also be able to provide such information (see the end of this article for contact information).

Other Requirements
It takes a certain kind of person to succeed in social services. According to Sheri Flanigan, "Social services are notoriously understaffed, so you also have to be willing to do the work (answer the phone, make copies, etc.). Even though you shouldn't be doing these things for a large portion of the day as a director, you have to be willing to work side by side with the other staff." Social services workers and directors also need to be emotionally stable, objective about situations they face, and responsible.

EXPLORING

The best way of exploring this field is by doing volunteer work for a nonprofit social service organization such as a hospice, shelter, or community outreach organization. Volunteering will give you exposure to the work environment as well as the situations an organization's clients face and help you develop your listening and communications skills. It can also give you an understanding of the way nonprofits work and the kind of expectations employers will have.

EMPLOYERS

Nonprofit social service organizations vary in size, purpose, and location. There are large, national nonprofit youth advocacy agencies in the thick of policy issues in Washington, D.C., for example. On the other hand, there are hospices, shelters, and youth support centers in small, community-oriented settings. The nature of the work a director does may also vary, depending on the organization and its size, needs, goals, and board of directors. For example, some social welfare nonprofits focus on changing legislation or public perceptions of certain social issues. These organizations will work differently from those that focus more on working directly with those needing services.

STARTING OUT

With your BSW or MSW in hand, you should be able to find entry-level work in the social services field. Your college career services office will have contacts to get you started, and the contacts you've made through your professors and colleagues will be invaluable in referring you to vacant positions.

Many social service directors started their careers as volunteers, then, as employees, they worked their way up the ranks. Sheri Flanigan entered the field as a Volunteer to Service in America (VISTA) volunteer. "VISTA was an excellent way for me to become familiar with the social service organization without having to start at entry level. I believe that service corps is what you make of it. It is easy as a volunteer not to put a lot of effort into the job, but don't fall into that trap. It is an excellent time to explore your opportunities, and to put a lot of effort into making your project work."

ADVANCEMENT

As the director or executive director of an organization, it can be difficult to see advancement opportunities because these people are already at the top levels of their organizations. A director, however, may see advancement as broadening the goals of his or her organization, increasing funding, or raising public awareness about the issues the organization addresses. Directors can also advance by moving from one nonprofit to another, larger nonprofit agency. Sheri Flanigan has a recommendation: "Look to grow your organization. You start as the executive director of a small nonprofit organization and soon you're the executive director of a large nonprofit—an organization that you nurtured and grew. There is also the possibility of being hired at a larger organization or an organization more tailored to your interests."

EARNINGS

Salaries in nonprofit work are typically lower than those paid for comparable work in the for-profit sector. In addition, salaries in the nonprofit sector vary tremendously depending on the size, location, and purpose of the organization. Large, high-profile nonprofits with specialized staff and budgets in the millions of dollars, for example, may pay directors well over $100,000, but six-figure salaries are still the exception in this field. According to Salary.com, the median annual income in 2007 for social service directors was approximately $86,000. The lowest paid directors earned $64,644 and highest paid directors earned $108,999 or more. The *NonProfit Times,* which conducts periodic salary surveys, reports the average earnings for CEOs and executive directors at nonprofit social services and welfare organizations were approximately $100,118 in 2006. In addition to information on CEOs' pay, the survey also included earnings information for other top administrative positions. The survey showed the national average for development directors was $65,004; for program directors, $60,577; and for directors of volunteers, $38,423.

Additionally, the survey reported salaries varied depending on a specific organization's budget. The median salaries for executive directors of nonprofit organizations with annual budgets of $500,000 or less were $56,500 while the median salaries of executive directors of nonprofits with budgets of $1 million to $9.9 million were $90,413. Directors working for nonprofit organizations with budgets of $50 million or more reported average salaries of $207,145. It is important to keep in mind that the top director job is an advanced position. Those just starting out in the field will earn much less than CEOs. People in this field, however, find that they have the reward of emotional satisfaction not found in every job.

Nonprofit organizations often offer benefits packages that can't be beat. In most agencies, employees can expect liberal annual paid vacation days, generous sick leave, health and hospitalization insurance, retirement plans, and good personnel practices.

WORK ENVIRONMENT

Nonprofits make great employers because of the positive work environment that they promote; nonprofits are typically humanitarian, responsive to stress, and supportive emotionally. However, these organizations almost always are run on tight budgets, and directors may have to deal with the constant threat of cutbacks or even closure. This can be stressful, and the director must concentrate on the "business" aspect of the work by getting funding, keeping costs down, and meeting with legislators or potential donors. Directors interact with many different people throughout their workdays and must be able to handle a variety of social situations. The tone of the work environment—dedicated, creative, community-oriented—is often set by the director's actions. Working hard and long hours promotes commitment to the job by everyone.

OUTLOOK

According to the U.S. Department of Labor, numerous job opportunities will be available in social services through 2014. Overall employment in the social services industry is projected to grow faster than the average for all occupations. The expected rapid growth is due to expanding services for the elderly, the mentally and physically disabled, and families in crisis. Our nation's elderly comprise a rapidly expanding segment of the population that is likely to need a wide range of social services. The growing emphasis on providing home care services, enabling aging seniors to remain at home rather than relocate to costly skilled nursing facilities, will contribute to employment growth in the social services industry. A continuing influx of foreign-born nationals to this country will spur the demand for a range of social services, such as financial, relocation, and job training assistance. Child protective services and special groups, such as adults who were abused as children, are also on the rise. In addition, crime, juvenile delinquency, mental illness, developmental disabilities, AIDS, and individual and family crises will spur demand for social services. Every agency will need to be overseen by a capable and savvy director. Many job openings will also stem from the need to replace nonprofit social service directors who leave their positions.

FOR MORE INFORMATION

This alliance of colleges, universities, and nonprofit organizations prepares undergraduates for careers with youth and human services agencies. For more information, contact
American Humanics
1100 Walnut Street, Suite 1900
Kansas City, MO 64106-2239
Tel: 816-561-6415
http://www.humanics.org

For a list of regulatory agencies or for a comparison of state regula-tions regarding licensing, certification, and registration, contact
Association of Social Work Boards
400 South Ridge Parkway, Suite B
Culpeper, VA 22701-3791
Tel: 800-225-6880
Email: info@aswb.org
http://www.aswb.org

For information on social work careers and educational programs, contact
Council on Social Work Education
1725 Duke Street, Suite 500
Alexandria, VA 22314-3457
Tel: 703-683-8080
Email: info@cswe.org
http://www.cswe.org

To access the online publication Choices: Careers in Social Work, *check out the NASW's Web site.*
National Association of Social Workers (NASW)
750 First Street, NE, Suite 700

Washington, DC 20002-4241
Tel: 202-408-8600
http://www.naswdc.org

For information on student memberships, scholarships, and master's degree programs in human services, visit the NOHS' Web site.
National Organization for Human Services (NOHS)
90 Madison Street, Suite 206
Denver, CO 80206-5418
Tel: 303-320-5430
http://www.nationalhumanservices.org

For information on volunteer opportunities, visit
AmeriCorps*VISTA (Volunteers In Service To America)
http://www.americorps.org/about/programs/vista.asp

For more information on nonprofits, contact
Independent Sector
http://independentsector.org

INTERVIEW

Vesna Stelcer *is the executive director of The MGR Foundation (http://mgrf.org) in Chicago, Illinois.* She *discussed her career with the editors of* Careers in Focus: Nonprofit Organizations.

Q. Please tell us about your organization.
A. The MGR Foundation is a public nonprofit that provides direct service to the community. It is committed to overcoming social and economic barriers and creating innovative programs that positively impact our communities.

Q. What are your primary and secondary duties?
A. My overarching role is to be the caretaker of the organization. My primary duties consist of creating and maintaining relationships with funders, donors, supporters, partners, and volunteers; inspiring and managing staff; keeping board members informed and involved; raising money; and serving as event coordinator, public relations specialist, and human resources specialist.

My secondary duties include keeping aware of trends in the nonprofit sector (changing community needs, shifting revenue sources, etc.); monitoring the organization's internal needs;

managing funds; evaluating on an ongoing basis the effectiveness of the organization; and fulfilling our mission.

Q. What do you like most and least about your job?
A. The most rewarding part of my job is directly working with the individuals that we serve in the community (tutoring, volunteering, running, acting, communicating, and just being).

What do I like the least? Nothing. I truly love every aspect of my job and consider myself extremely fortunate to be in the position that I am to effect change.

Q. What advice would you give to high school students who are interested in entering nonprofit careers?
A. Be diligent in doing research about what you are most interested in accomplishing—be an intern, volunteer, or whatever it takes to understand the environment you wish to pursue. Above all else, follow your heart and passion.

Orientation and Mobility Specialists

QUICK FACTS

School Subjects
Health
Psychology

Personal Skills
Communication/ideas
Helping/teaching

Work Environment
Primarily indoors
Primarily multiple locations

Minimum Education Level
Bachelor's degree

Salary Range
$27,280 to $43,040 to
$64,070+

Certification or Licensing
Required by certain states

Outlook
Faster than the average

DOT
076

GOE
14.06.01

NOC
4215

O*NET-SOC
N/A

OVERVIEW

Orientation and mobility specialists help people with disabilities stay actively involved in society. They teach blind, visually impaired, and disabled individuals how to master the skills necessary to live independently and often encourage them to participate in various educational or recreational programs. Specialists also serve as a source of information, referring clients to financial aid, benefits, and legal advice. These workers may be employed directly by an individual or indirectly through community planning, research, and publicity projects.

HISTORY

Helping those with disabilities has long been a part of the social work profession. As early as 1657, facilities called almshouses provided shelter, food, and work to the poor and those with disabilities. In the mid-1800s, middle-class women referred to as "friendly visitors" visited the homes of poor families to instruct the disabled in household management, the pursuit of employment, and the education of children. However, these friendly visitors and other early charitable organizations were sometimes limited in whom they would serve, often providing help and information only to those with their same moral views and religious backgrounds.

People with severe disabilities were often confined to institutions. By the late 18th century, many states and counties had built these facilities, then referred to as insane asylums, for the 24-hour care of people suffering from afflictions ranging from mental retardation to paralysis. The patients of these hospitals were often committed against their will by relatives. Few efforts were made to help patients return to society to lead normal, active lives.

The settlement houses of the late 19th century, such as Jane Addams's Hull House of Chicago, led to the development of more sensitive and enlightened ways to help people. Social workers lived among the residents, listening and learning along with them. But even with this new understanding of social work, those with disabilities were still unable to get complete assistance. Society wanted to help those in need but didn't necessarily want to live among them. As a result, separate schools, workplaces, and agencies for the disabled were established. Although social workers instructed blind people in how to cook and clean, how to use a guide dog, and how to read braille, they made few efforts to integrate them into the community.

Legal efforts to end this discrimination began in 1920 with the passing of the Vocational Rehabilitation Act. This act led to the development of state and federal agencies focused on enhancing the employment opportunities for people with disabilities. Over the years, this act has broadened to include job counseling and retraining services and the provision of prosthetic and other assisting devices. More recent efforts toward ending discrimination in employment and public services include the passing of the Americans with Disabilities Act of 1990.

THE JOB

Although he was diagnosed with multiple sclerosis years ago, Ken Smith has only recently required the use of a wheelchair. He also has only partial use of his right hand. For the last few years, he has worked as a newspaper journalist, driving himself to crime scenes, taking notes during interviews, and writing at a frantic pace to keep up with the pace of the newsroom. Now that he requires a wheelchair to get around, he is going to have to make many adjustments in his life. Fortunately for Smith, there are a number of services and benefits to help him; he just needs to know how to find this help.

The simple act of providing information is one of the most important jobs of an orientation and mobility specialist. These workers help to direct people like Smith to the many agencies available that assist those with vision and mobility impairments. By listening carefully to the problem, orientation and mobility specialists determine the best route for assistance, contact the agency on behalf of the client, and make sure the client receives the proper assistance. Because of limited funding and support, disability services are often unable to promote themselves. The biggest problem facing communities is not the lack of services available, but the lack of public awareness of these outlets.

However, Smith will require much more than names and phone numbers from an orientation and mobility specialist. He not only needs to find the right wheelchair, but he also needs instruction on how to use it. His home needs to be analyzed to determine what modifications need to be made (for example, wheelchair ramps, handrails, and wider doorways). If the necessary modifications cannot be made, he will have to consider moving to a new place. For all of these somewhat daunting decisions, Smith can ask an orientation and mobility specialist for advice.

Smith's workplace may also require modifications. Though perfectly capable of continuing his work as a journalist, he is going to have to fulfill his duties in different ways. For example, a special car may be required. Because of the limited use of his hand, he may need a modified computer keyboard or an assistant. An orientation and mobility specialist can serve as a client's advocate, negotiating with employers to prevent any cause for discrimination in the workplace. Specialists may also offer training and education programs to integrate or reintegrate the client into the workplace.

An orientation and mobility specialist also serves as a counselor. A client may need individual therapy or a support group. The family of the client may also need counseling on how to adjust to a parent's or child's disability.

In addition to offering services that directly benefit the client (counseling, advocacy, education, and referral), some specialists may offer services that have indirect benefits for clients. These additional services include outreach, publicity, planning, and research. Because of a general lack of awareness of the social services available, orientation and mobility specialists may focus on ways to educate the public about the challenges facing those with disabilities. They may lead fund-raising efforts for research or programs aimed at assisting the disabled community.

REQUIREMENTS

High School

Because you will need a college degree and a well-rounded education, take your high school's program of college preparatory classes. These classes should include math and science courses as well as a foreign language. Strong communication skills are needed for this work, so to improve your skills in this area, take four years of English. Speech and journalism classes are also beneficial. Courses in history, social studies, sociology, and psychology are also recommended.

Because a large part of the job is providing information about disability services, you should be comfortable using the Internet and various computer programs. Not only will you have to be able to work with computers yourself, you may be required to teach clients how to use them, too.

Postsecondary Training
The Association for Education and Rehabilitation of the Blind and Visually Impaired (commonly known as AER) provides a listing of approved orientation and mobility programs at the graduate, under-graduate, and certification-only levels. Programs include instruction in mobility techniques, where students simulate blindness or limited vision with blindfolds or other devices. Internships with disability agencies are also incorporated into the programs.

Other specialists prepare themselves for the career by studying social work. The Council on Social Work Education requires that five areas be covered in accredited bachelor's degree social work pro-grams: human behavior and the social environment, social welfare policy and services, social work practice, research, and field practi-cum. Most programs require two years of liberal arts study, followed by two years of study in the social work major. Also, students must complete a field practicum of at least 400 hours.

Though some starting positions require only a bachelor's degree, most supervisory and administrative positions within social work require further education. Graduate programs are organized accord-ing to fields of practice (e.g., mental health care), problem areas (e.g., substance abuse), population groups (e.g., the elderly), and prac-tice roles (e.g., practice with individuals, families, or communities). They are usually two-year programs with at least 900 hours of field practice. Doctoral degrees are also available for those interested in research, planning, or community outreach jobs.

Certification or Licensing
Only selected states require orientation and mobility specialists to be certified. The Academy for Certification of Vision Rehabilitation and Education Professionals offers certification for orientation and mobility specialists who meet certain educational and experience requirements. To be eligible to sit for the certification exam, individ-uals must first complete an AER-approved orientation and mobility program. Applicants who meet these certification requirements can use the designation, certified orientation and mobility specialist.

Other Requirements

For years, people with disabilities have faced discrimination. This discrimination is fueled by fear, by misunderstanding, and by the way people with disabilities are represented in popular culture. Orientation and mobility specialists must be able to honestly address their own perceptions of people with disabilities. Specialists must be sensitive to the client's situation and have a genuine interest in involving that person in the community and workplace.

Specialists also work frequently with the elderly, which requires understanding the aging experience. Workers must be patient and be good listeners to provide the elderly with the supportive network they need.

Communication skills are also very important. Much of the work as an orientation and mobility specialist involves talking and listening to clients, teaching, interviewing, and counseling. You will need to provide clear instructions to clients, their families, and their employers.

Because many of the problems facing those with disabilities stem from discrimination, many specialists work to educate the public about living with disabilities through research, reports, and fundraising. Being comfortable talking to a variety of people and in a variety of settings is an asset for these specialists.

EXPLORING

To learn more about this work, you can explore Web sites concerning disabilities and social work. A job in the school or public library helping people conduct research will put your information retrieval skills to good use. Working on the school newspaper will also help you develop your writing, researching, and interviewing skills, all important aspects of social work.

Part-time data entry jobs at a hospital or long-term care facility can familiarize you with medical terminology and the services available to people with disabilities. A part-time job in a retail pharmacy will involve you directly with people with disabilities and also the services that pay for the rental and purchase of wheelchairs, walkers, and canes. You can also gain experience by volunteering at any social service agency to get a sense of the work environment and responsibilities.

EMPLOYERS

Orientation and mobility specialists can find work with for-profit, nonprofit, and public programs. They may work in hospitals and community agencies such as transitional living services or with private agencies that focus on providing services specifically to those with disabilities.

An orientation and mobility specialist may also be self-employed, providing service on a contract basis to individuals or social service agencies.

STARTING OUT

To gain experience in social work, consider working with a social service agency specializing in information and referral. Rehabilitation centers, senior homes, schools, and summer camps for the blind, visually impaired, and disabled also offer many opportunities for experience. Because of limited funding, staffing may consist of only a few social work professionals, and the rest may be volunteers or assistants. Volunteer work may lead to full-time employment or simply introduce you to other social work professionals who can provide career guidance and letters of reference.

ADVANCEMENT

Orientation and mobility specialists may advance to become supervisors of assistants or executive directors of rehabilitation agencies. Another possible route for advancement is through teaching.

The more challenging and better-paying jobs tend to go to those with more years of practical experience and higher degrees. Further study, extensive experience, and good references will lead to advancement in the profession. Also, many social work programs offer continuing education workshops, courses, and seminars. These refresher courses help practicing specialists refine their skills and learn about new areas of practice, methods, and problems. These courses are intended to supplement previous education, not substitute for a bachelor's or master's degree. Continuing education can lead to job promotions and salary increases.

EARNINGS

The higher the degree held by specialists, the higher their earning potential. Those with a Ph.D. can take jobs in indirect service, research, and planning. Salaries also vary among regions; in general, social workers on the East and West Coasts earn higher salaries than those in the Midwest. During the first five years of practice, salaries increase faster than in later years.

Medical and public health social workers earned a median annual salary of $43,040 in 2006, according to the U.S. Department of Labor. The lowest paid 10 percent earned less than $27,280 and the highest paid 10 percent earned more than $64,070.

Specialists who work in school systems are generally paid on the same scale as teachers in the system. Those who work for private clients are usually paid by the hour or per session.

WORK ENVIRONMENT

Orientation and mobility specialists work part of the time in an office, analyzing and updating client files, interviewing clients over the phone, and talking with other service agencies. Depending on the size of the agency, office duties such as typing letters, filing, and answering phones may be performed by an aide or volunteer.

The rest of their time is spent outside the office, interacting directly with clients and others. Orientation and mobility specialists are involved directly with the people they serve and must carefully examine their clients' living conditions and family relations.

Advocacy involves work in a variety of different environments; it involves meetings with clients' employers, agency directors, and local legislators. Should the client press charges for discrimination, orientation and mobility specialists may be called upon to testify in court.

Both counseling and advocacy can be stressful aspects of the work, but helping to empower people with disabilities can be very rewarding.

OUTLOOK

According to the American Association of People with Disabilities, more than 56 million people (nearly one out of every five Americans) have a disability. In addition to continuing the fight against discrimination in the workplace and in general society, the disabled also need assistance in order to live productive lives.

Future funding is an important consideration for social service agencies. In many cases, the agencies providing information and referral must compete for funding with the very programs to which they refer people. This calls for good relationships between agencies and services. In order for agencies to receive adequate funding, social workers, including orientation and mobility specialists, must conduct research and provide reports to federal, state, and local governments showing proof of financial need. Their reports help to illustrate where funds should be allocated to best serve the disabled community.

According to the U.S. Department of Labor, the employment of social workers, including those who work with the visually and physically impaired, is expected to increase faster than the average for all occupations through 2014. Specialists will continue to increase public awareness of the importance of aid for the disabled and visually impaired. Assistance services will continue to make their way into more public areas, such as libraries, workplaces, and other public facilities.

New computer technology will continue to cater to the special needs of the disabled. The development of specialized equipment and the expansion of Internet resources allow the disabled and visually impaired to access online resources for assistance. Orientation and mobility specialists will be needed to help those with disabilities use new technology to their best advantage.

FOR MORE INFORMATION

For information on certification, contact
**Academy for Certification of Vision Rehabilitation and
    Education Professionals**
3333 North Campbell Avenue, Suite 11
Tucson, AZ 85719-2362
Tel: 520-887-6816
Email: info@acvrep.org
http://www.acvrep.org

For resources and advocacy for the disabled community, contact
American Association of People with Disabilities
1629 K Street, NW, Suite 503
Washington, DC 20006-1634
Tel: 800-840-8844
Email: aapd@aol.com
http://www.aapd.com

For information on educational programs, contact
**Association for Education and Rehabilitation of the Blind and
    Visually Impaired**
1703 North Beauregard Street, Suite 440
Alexandria, VA 22311-1744
Tel: 703-671-4500
http://www.aerbvi.org

To read frequently asked questions about how to become a social worker, check out the following Web site:
Council on Social Work Education
1725 Duke Street, Suite 500
Alexandria, VA 22314-3457
Tel: 703-683-8080
Email: info@cswe.org
http://www.cswe.org

For information about careers, education, and job leads, contact
National Association of Social Workers
750 First Street, NE, Suite 700
Washington, DC 20002-4241
Tel: 202-408-8600
http://www.socialworkers.org

For career information and job listings available in Canada, contact
Canadian Association of Social Workers
383 Parkdale Avenue, Suite 402
Ottawa, ON K1Y 4R4 Canada
Tel: 613-729-6668
http://www.casw-acts.ca

Psychologists

OVERVIEW

Psychologists teach, counsel, conduct research, or administer programs to understand people and help people understand themselves. Psychologists examine individual and group behavior through testing, experimenting, and studying personal histories.

Psychologists normally hold doctorates in psychology. Unlike psychiatrists, they are not medical doctors and cannot prescribe medication. Approximately 179,000 psychologists are employed in the United States.

HISTORY

The first syllable in psychology derives from *psyche,* a Greek word meaning soul. The second half of psychology contains the root of the word *logic.* Thus, psychology translates as "the science of the soul."

Early philosophers emphasized differences between body and soul. Plato, for example, believed they were two entirely different parts. Modern scholars tend to emphasize the unity between mind and body rather than their dissimilarity.

The founder of experimental psychology, Wilhelm Wundt, held both an M.D. and a Ph.D. A physician, he taught at the University of Leipzig, where his title was professor of philosophy. Like Wundt, German scholars of the 19th century were committed to the scientific method. Discovery by experiment was considered the only respectable way for learned thinkers to work. Thus it was not thought strange that in 1879, Wundt set up an experimental laboratory to conduct research upon human behavior. Many people who later became famous psychologists in the United States received their training under Wundt.

At the turn of the 20th century, Russian physiologist Ivan Pavlov discovered a key aspect of behaviorist theory while studying the process of digestion. While experimenting on dogs, he found that they began to salivate in anticipation of their food. He discovered that if he rang a bell before presenting their meat, the dogs associated the sound of a bell with mealtime. He then would ring the bell but withhold the food. The dogs' saliva flowed anyway, whether or not they saw or smelled food. Pavlov called this substitute stimulus a "conditioned response." Many psychologists began to incorporate the theory of conditioned response into their theories of learning.

One of the most famous pioneers in psychology was Sigmund Freud, whose work led to many of the modern theories of behavior. Freud lived and practiced in Vienna, Austria, until Hitler's forces caused him to flee to England. His work on the meaning of dreams, the unconscious, and the nature of various emotional disturbances has had a profound effect upon the profession and practice of psychology for more than 60 years, although many psychologists now disagree with some of his theories.

Many Americans have contributed greatly to the science that seeks to understand human behavior: William James, Robert Woodworth, E. L. Thorndike, Clark Hull, B. F. Skinner, and others.

THE JOB

Psychology is both a science and a profession. As a science, it is a systematic approach to the understanding of people and their behavior; as a profession, it is the application of that understanding to help solve human problems. Psychology is a rapidly growing field, and psychologists work on a great variety of problems.

The field of psychology is so vast that no one person can become an expert in all of its specialties. The psychologist usually concentrates on one specialty. Many specialists use overlapping methodologies, theories, and treatments.

Many psychologists teach some area of basic psychology in colleges and universities. They are also likely to conduct research and supervise graduate student work in an area of special interest.

Clinical psychologists concern themselves with people's mental and emotional disorders. They assess and treat problems ranging from normal psychological crises, such as adolescent rebellion or middle-age loss of self-esteem, to extreme conditions, such as severe depression and schizophrenia.

Some clinical psychologists work almost exclusively with children. They may be staff members at a child guidance clinic or a treatment center for children at a large general hospital. *Child psychologists* and other clinical psychologists may engage in private practice, seeing clients at offices. Clinical psychologists comprise the largest group of specialists.

Developmental psychologists study how people develop from birth through old age. They describe, measure, and explain age-related changes in behavior, stages of emotional development, universal traits and individual differences, and abnormal changes in development. Many developmental psychologists teach and do research in colleges and universities. Some specialize in programs for children in day care centers, preschools, hospitals, or clinics. Others specialize in programs for the elderly.

Social psychologists study how people interact with one other, and how individuals are affected by their environment. Social psychology has developed from four sources: sociology, cultural anthropology, psychiatry, and psychology. Social psychologists are interested in individual and group behavior. They study the ways groups influence individuals and vice versa. They study different kinds of groups: ethnic, religious, political, educational, family, and many others. The social psychologist has devised ways to research group nature, attitudes, leadership patterns, and structure.

Counseling psychologists work with people who have problems they find difficult to face alone. These clients are not usually mentally or emotionally ill, but they are emotionally upset, anxious, or struggling with some conflict within themselves or their environment. By helping people solve their problems, make decisions, and cope with everyday stresses, the counseling psychologist actually is working in preventive mental health.

School psychologists frequently do diagnosis and remediation. They may engage primarily in preventive and developmental psychology. Many school psychologists are assigned the duty of testing pupils surmised to be exceptional. Other school psychologists work almost entirely with children who have proven to be a problem to themselves or to others and who have been referred for help by teachers or other members of the school system. Many school psychologists are concerned with pupils who reveal various kinds of learning disabilities. School psychologists may also be called upon to work with relationship problems between parents and children.

Industrial-organizational psychologists are concerned with the relation between people and work. They deal with organizational structure, worker productivity, job satisfaction, consumer behavior, personnel training and development, and the interaction between humans and machines.

Psychometrists work with intelligence, personality, and aptitude tests used in clinics, counseling centers, schools, and businesses. They administer tests, score them, and interpret results as related to standard norms. Psychometrists also study methods and techniques used to acquire and evaluate psychological data. They may devise new, more reliable tests. These specialists are usually well trained in mathematics, statistics, and computer programming and technology.

The *educational psychologist* is concerned primarily with how people teach, learn, and evaluate learning. Many educational psychologists are employed on college or university faculties, and they also conduct research into learning theory. Educational psychologists are also interested in the evaluation of learning.

Experimental psychologists conduct scientific experiments on particular aspects of behavior, either animal or human. Much experimental study is done in learning, in physiological psychology (the relationship of behavior to physiological processes), and in comparative psychology (sometimes called animal psychology). Many experimental psychological studies are carried out with animals, partly because their environments can be carefully controlled.

Many psychologists of all kinds find that writing skills are helpful. They may write up the results of research efforts for a scholarly journal. Psychologists prepare papers for presentation at professional association meetings and sometimes write books or articles. As consultants or industrial psychologists, they may write instruction manuals. Educational psychologists may prepare test manuals.

Some psychologists become administrators who direct college or university psychology departments or personnel services programs in a school system or industry. Some become agency or department directors of research in scientific laboratories. They may be promoted to department head in a state or federal government agency. *Chief psychologists* in hospitals or psychiatric centers plan psychological treatment programs, direct professional and nonprofessional personnel, and oversee psychological services provided by the institution.

REQUIREMENTS

High School

Because you will need to continue your education beyond high school in order to become a psychologist, you should enroll in college preparatory courses. Your class schedule should concentrate on English, computer science, mathematics, and sciences. Algebra, geometry, and calculus are important to take, as are biology, chemistry, and physics. You should take social science courses, such as psychology and sociology. You should also take a modern foreign language, such as French or German, because reading comprehension of these languages is one of the usual requirements for obtaining the doctorate degree.

Postsecondary Training

A doctorate in psychology (Ph.D. or Psy.D.) is recommended. While most new doctorates in the psychology field received a Ph.D., the number of Psy.D. recipients has more than doubled—to 16 percent—over the past decade. Some positions are available to people with a master's degree, but they are jobs of lesser responsibility and lower salaries than those open to people with a doctorate.

Psychology is an obvious choice for your college major, but not all graduate programs require entering students to have a psychology bachelor's degree. Nevertheless, your college studies should include a number of psychology courses, such as experimental psychology, developmental psychology, and abnormal psychology. You should also take classes in statistics as well as such classes as English, foreign language, and history to complete a strong liberal arts education.

Master's degree programs typically take two years to complete. Course work at this level usually involves statistics, ethics, and industrial and organizational content. If you want to work as a school psychologist, you will need to complete a supervised, yearlong internship at a school after receiving your degree.

Some doctoral programs accept students with master's degrees; in other cases, students enter a doctoral program with only a bachelor's degree. Because entrance requirements vary, you will need to research the programs you are interested in to find out their specific requirements. The doctorate degree typically takes between four and seven years to complete for those who begin their studies with only the bachelor's degree. Coursework will include studies in various areas of psychology and research (including work in quantitative research methods). Those who focus on research often complete a yearlong postdoctoral fellowship. Those who want to work as clinical, counseling, or school psychologists must complete a one-year supervised internship. Frequently those who are interested in clinical, counseling, or school psychology will get the Psy.D., because this degree emphasizes clinical rather than research work. In addition, those interested in these three areas should attend a program accredited by the American Psychological Association (APA).

Unlike psychiatrists, psychologists do not need to attend medical school.

Certification or Licensing

The American Board of Professional Psychology offers voluntary specialty certification in a number of areas, including clinical psychology, clinical neuropsychology, and counseling, forensic, organizational and business, rehabilitation, and school psychology. Requirements for certification include having a doctorate in psychology, professional experience, appropriate postdoctoral training, and the passing of an examination. Those who fulfill these requirements receive the designation of diplomate.

The National Association of School Psychologists awards the nationally certified school psychologist designation to applicants who complete educational requirements, an internship, and pass an examination.

Psychologists in independent practice or those providing any type of patient care, such as clinical, counseling, and school psychologists, must be licensed or certified by the state in which they practice. Some states require the licensing of industrial/organizational psychologists. Because requirements vary, you will need to check with your state's licensing board for specific information. About 26 states recognize the nationally certified school psychologist (NCSP) designation, awarded by the National Association of School Psychologists.

Other Requirements

Because psychology is such a broad field, various personal attributes apply to different psychology positions. Those involved in research, for example, should be analytical, detail oriented, and have strong math and writing skills. Those working with patients should be "people persons," able to relate to others, and have excellent listening skills. No matter what their area of focus, however, all psychologists should be committed to lifelong learning since our understanding of humans is constantly evolving.

EXPLORING

If you are interested in psychology, explore the field by taking psychology classes in high school and reading all you can about the subject, including biographies of and works by noted psychologists. In addition, make an appointment to talk about the profession with a psychologist who may work at a nearby school, college, hospital, or clinic. Use the Internet to learn more about mental health issues by visiting Web sites, such as that of Mental Health America at http://www.nmha.org or the APA at http://www.apa.org.

If being involved with patient care interests you, gain experience in the health care field by volunteering at a local hospital or clinic. In addition, volunteer opportunities may exist at local nursing homes, where you will also have the chance to work with clients needing some type of assistance. If doing research work sounds appealing to you, consider joining your school's science club, which may offer the opportunity to work on projects, document the process, and work as part of a team.

EMPLOYERS

Approximately 179,000 psychologists are employed in the United States. About 4 out of 10 psychologists are self-employed. Clinical psychologists may teach at colleges or universities. Or, clinical psychologists may work with patients in a private practice or a hospital, where they provide therapy after evaluation through special tests.

Many developmental psychologists teach and research in colleges and universities. Some specialize in programs for children in day care centers, preschools, hospitals, or clinics.

Social psychologists often teach and conduct research in colleges or universities. They also work for agencies of the federal or state government or in private research firms. Some work as consultants. An increasing number of social psychologists work as researchers and personnel managers in such nontraditional settings as advertising agencies, corporations, and architectural and engineering firms.

Counseling psychologists work in college or university counseling centers; they also teach in psychology departments. They may be in

Books to Read

Eberts, Marjorie, and Margaret Gisler. *Careers for Good Samaritans and Other Humanitarian Types.* 3d ed. New York: McGraw-Hill, 2006.

McKinney, Anne, ed. *Real Resumes for Jobs in Nonprofit Organizations.* Fayetteville, N.C.: Prep Publishing, 2004.

Otting, Laura Gassner. *Change Your Career: Transitioning to the Nonprofit Sector.* New York: Kaplan Publishing, 2007.

Slesinger, Larry. *Search: Winning Strategies to Get Your Next Job in the Nonprofit World.* Glen Echo, Md.: Piemonte Press, 2004.

WetFeet. *Careers in Nonprofits and Government Agencies.* San Francisco: WetFeet, 2005.

private practice. Or they may work at a community health center, a marriage counseling agency, or a federal agency such as the Department of Veterans Affairs.

Consumer psychologists study consumer reactions to products or services. They are hired by advertising, promotion, and packaging companies.

Psychometrists may be employed in colleges and universities, testing companies, private research firms, or government agencies.

Educational psychologists may work for test publishing firms devising and standardizing tests of ability, aptitude, personal preferences, attitudes, or characteristics.

STARTING OUT

Those entering the field with only a bachelor's degree will face strong competition for few jobs. The university career services office or a psychology professor may be able to help such a student find a position assisting a psychologist at a health center or other location. Positions beyond the assistant level, however, will be very difficult to attain. Those graduating from master's or doctorate degree programs will find more employment opportunities. Again, university career services offices may be able to provide these graduates with assistance. In addition, contacts made during an internship may offer job leads. Joining professional organizations and networking with members is also a way to find out about job openings. In addition, these organizations, such as the APA, often list job vacancies in their publications for members.

ADVANCEMENT

For those who have bachelor's or master's degrees, the first step to professional advancement is to complete a doctorate degree. After that, advancement will depend on the area of psychology in which the person is working. For example, a psychologist teaching at a college or university may advance through the academic ranks from instructor to professor. Some college teachers who enjoy administrative work become department heads.

Psychologists who work for state or federal government agencies may, after considerable experience, be promoted to head a section or department. School psychologists might become directors of pupil personnel services. Industrial psychologists can rise to managerial or administrative positions.

After several years of experience, many psychologists enter private practice or set up their own research or consulting firms.

EARNINGS

Because the psychology field offers so many different types of employment possibilities, salaries for psychologists vary greatly. In addition, the typical conditions affecting salaries, such as the person's level of education, professional experience, and location, also apply. The U.S. Department of Labor reports that salaries for clinical, counseling, and school psychologists ranged from less than $35,280 to $102,730 or more in 2006 while salaries for industrial and organizational psychologists ranged from $48,380 or less to $139,620 or more. According to *Compensation in Nonprofit Organizations 2006*, a report from Abbott, Langer & Associates, psychologists had median annual incomes of $60,132 in 2006.

WORK ENVIRONMENT

Psychologists work under many different conditions. Those who work as college or university teachers usually have offices in a building on campus and access to a laboratory in which they carry out experiments.

Offices of school psychologists may be located in the school system headquarters. They may see students and their parents at those offices, or they might work in space set aside for them in several schools within the school district that they may visit regularly.

Psychologists in military service serve in this country or overseas. They may be stationed in Washington, D.C., and assigned to an office job, or they may be stationed with other military personnel at a post or, more likely, in a military hospital.

Psychologists employed in government work in such diverse places as public health or vocational rehabilitation agencies, the Department of Veterans Affairs, the Peace Corps, the Department of Education, or a state department of education. Their working conditions depend largely on the kind of jobs they have. They may be required to travel a lot or to produce publications. They may work directly with people or be assigned entirely to research.

Some psychologists are self-employed. Most work as clinical psychologists and have offices where they see clients individually. Others work as consultants to business firms. Self-employed psychologists rent or own their office spaces and arrange their own work schedules.

To be a psychologist, one must have a desire to help people understand themselves and others. A basic curiosity is required as well as a fascination with the way the human mind works.

OUTLOOK

The U.S. Department of Labor projects that employment for psychologists will grow faster than the average for all occupations through 2014, with the largest increase in schools, hospitals, social service agencies, mental health centers, substance abuse treatment clinics, consulting firms, and private companies. Increased emphasis on health maintenance and illness prevention as well as growing interest in psychological services for special groups, such as children or the elderly, will create demand for psychologists. Many of these areas depend on government funding, however, and could be adversely affected in an economic downswing when spending is likely to be curtailed. Many openings should be available in business and industry, and the outlook is very good for psychologists who are in full-time independent practice.

Prospects look best for those with doctorates in applied areas, such as clinical, counseling, health, industrial/organizational, and school psychology, and for those with extensive technical training in quantitative research methods and computer applications. Postdoctorates are becoming increasingly crucial in the fields of research psychology that deal with behavior based on biology.

Competition for jobs will be tougher for those with master's or bachelor's degrees. Most job candidates with bachelor's degrees, in fact, will not be able to find employment in the psychology field beyond assistant-level jobs at such places as rehabilitation centers. Some may work as high school psychology teachers if they meet state teaching certification requirements.

FOR MORE INFORMATION

For information on specialty certification, contact
American Board of Professional Psychology
300 Drayton Street, 3rd Floor
Savannah, GA 31401-4443
Tel: 800-255-7792
Email: office@abpp.org
http://www.abpp.org

For more on careers in psychology and mental health issues, contact
American Psychological Association
750 First Street, NE
Washington, DC 20002-4242
Tel: 800-374-2721
http://www.apa.org

For licensing information, visit the following Web site:
Association of State and Provincial Psychology Boards
PO Box 241245
Montgomery, AL 36124-1245
Tel: 334-832-4580
Email: asppb@asppb.org
http://www.asppb.org

For more information on certification and becoming a school psychologist, including graduate school information, contact
National Association of School Psychologists
4340 East West Highway, Suite 402
Bethesda, MD 20814-4468
Tel: 301-657-0270
Email: center@nasweb.org
http://www.nasponline.org

For a list of graduate psychology programs in Canada, contact
Canadian Psychological Association
141 Laurier Avenue West, Suite 702
Ottawa, Ontario K1P 5J3 Canada
Tel: 613-237-2144
Email: cpa@cpa.ca
http://www.cpa.ca

For a whimsical introduction to psychology, visit
ePsych
http://epsych.msstate.edu

Public Interest Lawyers

QUICK FACTS

School Subjects
English
Government
Speech

Personal Skills
Communication/ideas
Leadership/management

Work Environment
Primarily indoors
Primarily multiple locations

Minimum Education Level
Master's degree

Salary Range
$40,000 to $52,000 to
$65,000+

Certification or Licensing
Required

Outlook
About as fast as the average

DOT
110

GOE
04.02.01

NOC
4112

O*NET-SOC
23-1011.00

OVERVIEW

Lawyers, or *attorneys*, help clients know their rights under the law and then help them achieve these rights before a judge, jury, government agency, or other legal forum, such as an arbitration panel. Lawyers represent individuals and for-profit and nonprofit organizations. Lawyers often choose a field of law in which to specialize. Lawyers specializing in public interest law provide a wide range of services to those who otherwise could not afford legal representation. They also work for organizations advocating for a particular cause. Their work is often done *pro bono*—for the public good—voluntarily and without payment. The American Bar Association, the largest association for legal professionals, has a Standing Committee on Pro Bono and Public Service. Approximately 735,000 lawyers work in the United States today in various legal specialties.

HISTORY

The tradition of governing people by laws has been established over centuries. Societies have built up systems of law that have been studied and drawn upon by later governments. The earliest known law is the Code of Hammurabi, developed about 1800 b.c. by the ruler of the Sumerians. Another early set of laws was the Law of Moses, known as the Ten Commandments. Every set of laws, no matter when they were introduced, has been accompanied by the need for someone to explain those laws and help others live under them.

The great orators of ancient Greece and Rome set up schools for young boys to learn by apprenticeship the many skills involved in pleading a law case. To be an eloquent speaker was the greatest advantage. The legal profession has matured since those earlier times; a great deal of training and an extensive knowledge of legal matters are required of the modern lawyer and judge.

Much modern European law was organized and refined by legal experts assembled by Napoleon; their body of law was known as the Napoleonic Code. English colonists coming to America brought English common law, from which American laws have grown. In areas of the United States that were heavily settled by Spanish colonists, there are traces of Spanish law. As the population in the country grew, along with business, those who knew the law were in high demand. The two main kinds of law are *civil* and *criminal,* but many other specialty areas are also prevalent today. When our country was young, most lawyers were general law practitioners—they knew and worked with all the laws for their clients' sakes. Today, there are many more lawyers who specialize in areas such as tax law, corporate law, intellectual property law, and public interest law.

Public interest law in the United States developed in the late 1800s, according to the National Legal Aid & Defender Association. The German Society of New York founded what is considered to be the first civil legal assistance program for poor people in 1876. The organization was formed to protect the rights of recent German immigrants. Later, it expanded its services to advocate for other groups and was renamed the Legal Aid Society of New York in 1890. It is still serving the disadvantaged today.

In the early 1920s, the American Bar Association created the Special Committee on Legal Aid Work and encouraged other legal associations to do the same. By the 1950s, legal aid programs were available in nearly every major U.S. city.

In 1964, the U.S. government began providing federal funding for civil legal assistance to poor people, which created strong growth for public interest law organizations.

In 1986, students from 14 law schools created the National Association for Public Interest Law (now known as Equal Justice Works) to advance the profession of public interest law.

Today, public interest law is a popular and rewarding career option for lawyers who are interested in helping the disadvantaged attain better lives.

THE JOB

Public interest lawyers (PILs) may have different specialties, but all direct their services to a particular group of clients—those who may not have the means to pay for legal counsel. PILs often provide their services pro bono, for little or no fee. While the majority of their clients are individuals who are poor or on fixed incomes PILS may also do work for public interest groups with a range of advocacy issues (such as the environment, adoption, or immigration).

Many PILs work for government-funded legal aid clinics and offices. For example, lawyers working for the Migrant Farm Worker Division of Texas RioGrande Legal Aid (TRLA) provide legal assistance to seasonal or migrant agricultural workers, some with alien status. These workers are mostly of Latino heritage. The TRLA provides civil legal service at no cost; its funding comes from a combination of support from the federal government and private foundations. Lawyers employed by the TRLA represent the rights of their clients regarding housing, employment, public benefits, and civil rights issues. They may also propose changes in welfare training and educational materials and services to these migrant workers. Lawyers working in this capacity are paid an annual salary, though much less compared to attorneys employed at a private firm.

Public defenders can also be considered public interest lawyers. Low-income or indigent people charged with a crime are often assigned a public defender to assist with their legal defense. Public defender agencies, at the state and federal level, are supported by public funding. Full-time public defenders specialize in criminal law—offenses committed against society or the state, such as theft, murder, or arson. They interview clients and witnesses to ascertain facts in a case, correlate their findings with known cases, and prepare a case to defend a client against the charges made. They conduct a defense at the trial, examine witnesses, and summarize the case with a closing argument to a jury.

Other PILs choose to provide legal counsel or work as advocates for nonprofit organizations. For example, a public interest lawyer may serve as the director of legal services and advocacy for an HIV/AIDS organization. Duties for someone in this position might include influencing the policies and positions of the executive and legislative branches of the federal government regarding HIV/AIDS, monitoring HIV/AIDS issues and helping lead community alliances against the disease, and educating the public about political candidates' positions regarding HIV/AIDS. Other lawyers working for this advocacy group might provide legal representation, offer technical advice, and participate in interviews and forums about HIV/AIDS.

Lawyers employed at private legal firms may also practice public interest law. Many support the work of various organizations and charities by providing their legal expertise *pro bono*. In fact, the American Bar Association urges its members to render at least 50 hours of *pro bono publico* legal services a year.

REQUIREMENTS

High School

A high school diploma, a college degree, and three years of law school are minimum requirements for a law degree. A high school diploma is a first step on the ladder of education that a lawyer must climb. If you are considering a career in law, courses such as government, history, social studies, and economics provide a solid background for entering college-level courses. Speech courses are also helpful to build strong communication skills necessary for the profession. Also take advantage of any computer-related classes or experience you can get, because public interest lawyers often use technology to research and interpret the law, from surfing the Internet to searching legal databases.

Postsecondary Training

To enter any law school approved by the American Bar Association, you must satisfactorily complete at least three, and usually four, years of college work. Most law schools do not specify any particular courses for prelaw education. Usually a liberal arts track is most advisable, with courses in English, history, economics, social sciences, logic, and public speaking. A college student planning on specialization in a particular area of law, however, might also take courses significantly related to that area, such as economics or political science. Some students interested in careers in public law earn bachelor's degrees in nonprofit management or social work.

Those interested should contact several law schools to learn more about any requirements and to see if they will accept credits from the college the student is planning to attend.

Currently, 196 law schools in the United States are approved by the American Bar Association; others, many of them night schools, are approved by state authorities only. Most of the approved law schools, however, do have night sessions to accommodate part-time students. Part-time courses of study usually take four years.

Law school training consists of required courses such as legal writing and research, contracts, criminal law, constitutional law, torts, and property. The second and third years may be devoted to specialized courses of interest to the student, such as public interest law. The study of cases and decisions is of basic importance to the law student, who will be required to read and study thousands of these cases. A degree of juris doctor (J.D.) or bachelor of laws (LL.B.) is usually granted upon graduation. Some law students considering specialization, research, or teaching may go on for advanced study.

Most law schools require that applicants take the Law School Admission Test (LSAT), where prospective law students are tested on their critical thinking, writing, and reasoning abilities.

Certification or Licensing

Every state requires that lawyers be admitted to the bar of that state before they can practice. They require that applicants graduate from an approved law school and that they pass a written examination in the state in which they intend to practice. In a few states, graduates of law schools within the state are excused from these written examinations. After lawyers have been admitted to the bar in one state, they can practice in another state without taking a written examination if the states have reciprocity agreements; however, they will be required to meet certain state standards of good character and legal experience and pay any applicable fees.

Other Requirements

Successful public interest lawyers need to be effective communicators, work well with people, and be able to find creative solutions to problems. PILs must also be compassionate, with a strong desire to help others, especially the disadvantaged. Oftentimes PILs are not rewarded financially, but rather with the knowledge of helping those unable to help themselves.

EXPLORING

If you think a career as a public interest lawyer might be right up your alley, there are several ways you can find out more about it before making that final decision. First, sit in on a trial or two at your local or state courthouse. Write down questions you have and terms or actions you do not understand. Then, talk to your guidance counselor and ask for help in setting up a telephone or in-person interview with a lawyer. Ask questions and get the scoop on what the career is really all about. Also, talk to your guidance counselor or political science teacher about starting or joining a job-shadowing program. Job shadowing programs allow you to follow a person in a certain career around for a day or two to get an idea of what goes on in a typical day. You may even be invited to help out with a few minor duties.

You can also search the World Wide Web for general information about public interest lawyers and current court cases. After you have done some research and talked to a lawyer and you still think you are destined for law school, try to get a part-time job in a law office—preferably one that specializes in public interest law. Ask your guidance counselor for help.

If you are already in law school, you might consider becoming a student member of the American Bar Association. Student members receive *Student Lawyer,* a magazine that contains useful information for aspiring lawyers. Sample articles from the magazine can be read at http://www.abanet.org/lsd/stulawyer.

EMPLOYERS

Approximately 735,000 lawyers are employed in the United States. The list of employers is endless—ranging from government agencies, to nonprofit organizations, to advocacy groups. Organizations such as Equal Justice Works (http://www.equaljusticeworks.org) offer programs for lawyers to match their pro bono legal services to individuals or areas that need them most. Appleseed (http://appleseeds. net), another nonprofit group, provides a network of pro bono legal experts to help individuals throughout the United States attain the opportunity to live a just and productive life. Many private law firms also encourage their lawyers to provide pro bono work or volunteer in other capacities.

STARTING OUT

Beginning lawyers often work as law clerks or as assistants to senior lawyers doing research work and other routine tasks. After a few years of experience, they may be assigned their own cases; some may choose to go into private practice specializing in public interest law.

Many new lawyers are recruited by law firms or other employers directly from law school. Recruiters come to the school and interview possible hires. Other new graduates can get job leads from local and state bar associations.

ADVANCEMENT

Lawyers, if they choose to pursue the specialty of public interest law, can advance by being assigned more responsibilities within their organization or firm. They can lead entire projects, take on higher profile cases, or represent an advocacy group. Public defenders can be promoted from the state to the federal level.

EARNINGS

According to a 2006 salary survey by the National Association for Law Placement, public defenders earned a median entry-level salary of $43,300; with five years' experience, $54,672; and with

11 to 15 years' experience, $65,500. Lawyers with public interest organizations earned a median entry-level salary of $40,000; with five years' experience, $52,000; and with 11 to 15 years' experience, $65,000. Experienced public interest lawyers earn salaries that vary depending on the type, size, and location of their employer. PILs who are employed by government agencies typically earn more than those employed by nonprofit organizations or foundations.

WORK ENVIRONMENT

Offices and courtrooms are usually pleasant, although busy, places to work. Public interest lawyers also spend significant amounts of time in law libraries or record rooms, in the homes and offices of clients, and sometimes in the jail cells of clients or prospective witnesses. Many lawyers never work in a courtroom. Unless they are directly involved in litigation, they may never perform at a trial.

Some courts, such as small claims, family, or surrogate, may have evening hours to provide flexibility to the community. Criminal arraignments may be held at any time of the day or night. Court hours for most lawyers are usually regular business hours, with a one-hour lunch break. Often lawyers have to work long hours, spending evenings and weekends preparing cases and materials and working with clients. In addition to the work, the lawyer must always keep up with the latest developments in the profession. Also, it takes a long time to become a qualified lawyer, and it may be difficult to earn an adequate living until the lawyer gets enough experience to develop an established private practice.

Public interest lawyers who are employed at law firms must often work grueling hours to advance in the firm. Spending long weekend hours doing research and interviewing people should be expected.

OUTLOOK

According to the *Occupational Outlook Handbook,* employment for lawyers is expected to grow about as fast as the average for all occupations through 2014, but record numbers of law school graduates have created strong competition for jobs, even though the number of graduates has begun to level off. Continued population growth, typical business activities, and increased numbers of legal cases involving health care, antitrust, environmental, intellectual property, international law, elder law, and sexual harassment issues, among others, will create a steady demand for lawyers. Law services will be more accessible to the middle-income public with the popularity of prepaid legal services and clinics.

Despite the relatively low salaries earned by public interest lawyers, there is strong competition for these jobs. Most lawyers enter the specialty after several years practicing law and completing internships or fellowships in public interest law. Opportunities will be best with state and federal governments.

FOR MORE INFORMATION

For more information about public interest law, contact
American Bar Association
Standing Committee on Pro Bono and Public Service
Center for Pro Bono
321 North Clark Street
Chicago, IL 60610-4714
Tel: 312-988-5759
http://www.abanet.org/legalservices/probono/contact.html

For information on law schools, contact
Association of American Law Schools
1201 Connecticut Avenue, NW, Suite 800
Washington, DC 20036-2717
Tel: 202-296-8851
Email: aals@aals.org
http://www.aals.org

For information on choosing a law school, law careers, salaries, and alternative law careers, contact
National Association for Law Placement
1025 Connecticut Avenue, NW, Suite 1110
Washington, DC 20036-5413
Tel: 202-835-1001
Email: info@nalp.org
http://www.nalp.org

For more information about public interest law, contact the following organizations:
Equal Justice Works
2120 L Street, NW, Suite 450
Washington, DC 20037-1541
Tel: 202-466-3686
Email: mail@equaljusticeworks.org
http://www.equaljusticeworks.org

National Legal Aid & Defender Association
1140 Connecticut Avenue, NW, Suite 900
Washington, DC 20036-4019
Tel: 202-452-0620
Email: info@nlada.org
http://www.nlada.org

PSLawNet
1025 Connecticut Avenue, NW, Suite 1108
Washington, DC 20036-5405
Tel: 202-296-0076
Email: pslawnet@nalp.org
http://www.pslawnet.org

Public Relations Specialists

OVERVIEW

Public relations (PR) specialists develop and maintain programs that present a favorable public image for an individual or organization. They provide information to the target audience (generally, the public at large) about the client, its goals and accomplishments, and any further plans or projects that may be of public interest.

PR specialists may be employed by nonprofit organizations, corporations, government agencies, or almost any type of organization. Many PR specialists hold positions in public relations consulting firms or work for advertising agencies. There are approximately 188,000 public relations specialists in the United States.

HISTORY

The first public relations counsel was a reporter named Ivy Ledbetter Lee, who in 1906 was named press representative for a group of coalmine operators. Labor disputes were becoming a large concern of the operators, and they had run into problems because of their continued refusal to talk to the press and the hired miners. Lee convinced the mine operators to start responding to press questions and supply the press with information on the mine activities.

During and after World War II, the rapid advancement of communications techniques prompted firms to realize they needed professional help to ensure their messages were given proper public attention. Manufacturing firms that had turned their production

QUICK FACTS

School Subjects
Business
English
Journalism

Personal Skills
Communication/ideas
Leadership/management

Work Environment
Primarily indoors
One location with some
   travel

Minimum Education Level
Bachelor's degree

Salary Range
$28,080 to $52,038 to
   $89,220+

Certification or Licensing
Voluntary

Outlook
Faster than the average

DOT
165

GOE
13.01.01NOC
5124

O*NET-SOC
11-2031.00, 27-3031.00

facilities over to the war effort returned to the manufacture of peace-time products and enlisted the aid of public relations professionals to forcefully and convincingly bring products and the company name before the buying public.

Large business firms, labor unions, and service organizations, such as the American Red Cross, Boy Scouts of America, and the YMCA, began to recognize the value of establishing positive, healthy relationships with the public that they served and depended on for support. The need for effective public relations was often emphasized when circumstances beyond a company's or institution's control created unfavorable reactions from the public.

Public relations specialists must be experts at representing their clients before the media. The rapid growth of the public relations field since 1945 is testimony to the increased awareness in all industries of the need for professional attention to the proper use of media and the proper public relations approach to the many publics of a firm or an organization—customers, employees, stockholders, contributors, and competitors.

THE JOB

PR specialists are employed to do a variety of tasks. They may be employed primarily as writers, creating reports, news releases, and booklet texts. Others write speeches or create copy for radio, TV, or film sequences. These workers often spend much of their time contacting the press, radio, and TV as well as magazines on behalf of the employer. Some PR specialists work more as editors than writers, fact-checking and rewriting employee publications, newsletters, shareholder reports, and other management communications.

Specialists may choose to concentrate in graphic design, using their background knowledge of art and layout for developing brochures, booklets, and photographic communications. Other PR workers handle special events, such as fund-raisers, press parties, convention exhibits, open houses, or anniversary celebrations.

PR specialists must be alert to any and all company or institutional events that are newsworthy. They prepare news releases and direct them toward the proper media. Specialists working for nonprofit organizations are concerned with efforts that will promote interest and create goodwill for the organization. For example, a public relations specialist for a large foundation such as the Bill & Melinda Gates Foundation might tout the organization's funding of HIV/AIDS vaccine research, its development of charter schools in hurricane-ravaged New Orleans, or its creation of a pilot program to help families in crisis. A PR specialist for a small foundation might seek to tout its literacy programs in local public schools in order to raise public awareness and solicit donations to keep the program going.

A large firm may have a director of public relations who is a vice president of the company and in charge of a staff that includes writers, artists, researchers, and other specialists. Publicity for an individual or a small nonprofit organization may involve many of the same areas of expertise but may be carried out by a few people or possibly even one person.

Many PR workers act as consultants (rather than staff) of a nonprofit organization, corporation, association, college, hospital, or other institution. These workers have the advantage of being able to operate independently, state opinions objectively, and work with more than one type of business or association.

Public relations professionals may specialize. *Lobbyists* try to persuade legislators and other office holders to pass laws favoring the interests of the firms or people they represent. *Fund-raising directors* develop and direct programs designed to raise funds for social welfare agencies and other nonprofit organizations.

Early in their careers, public relations specialists become accustomed to having others receive credit for their behind-the-scenes work. The speeches they draft will be delivered by a foundation's executive director, the magazine articles they prepare may be credited to the president of the company or nonprofit organization, and they may be consulted to prepare the message to stockholders from the chairman of the board that appears in the annual report.

REQUIREMENTS

High School
While in high school, take courses in English, journalism, public speaking, humanities, and languages because public relations are based on effective communication with others. Courses such as these will develop your skills in written and oral communication as well as provide a better understanding of different fields and industries to be publicized.

Postsecondary Training
Most people employed in public relations service have a college degree. Major fields of study most beneficial to developing the proper skills are public relations, English, and journalism. Some employers feel that majoring in the area in which the public relations person will eventually work is the best training. Knowledge of business administration is most helpful as is a native talent for selling.

Average Salaries in Nonprofit Organizations

There are literally dozens of careers available in nonprofits. Here are some average salaries for jobs not included in this book:

Physician (general practice)	$143,307
Editor (books and periodicals)	$57,237
Human resources manager	$55,698
Computer systems analyst	$54,000
Registered nurse	$49,920
Computer programmer	$48,250
Accountant	$42,172
Curator	$40,583
Secretary	$28,195
Maintenance worker	$25,500

Source: *Compensation in Nonprofit Organizations 2006*, Abbott, Langer & Associates

A graduate degree may be required for managerial positions. People with a bachelor's degree in public relations can find staff positions with either an organization or a public relations firm.

More than 200 colleges and about 100 graduate schools offer degree programs or special courses in public relations. In addition, many other colleges offer at least courses in the field. Public relations programs are sometimes administered by the journalism or communication departments of schools. In addition to courses in theory and techniques of public relations, interested individuals may study organization, management and administration, and practical applications and often specialize in areas such as business, government, and nonprofit organizations. Other preparation includes courses in creative writing, psychology, communications, advertising, and journalism.

Certification or Licensing
The Public Relations Society of America and the International Association of Business Communicators accredit public relations workers who have at least five years of experience in the field and pass a comprehensive examination. Such accreditation is a sign of competence in this field, although it is not a requirement for employment.

Other Requirements

Today's public relations specialist must be a businessperson first, both to understand how to perform successfully in business and to comprehend the needs and goals of the organization or client. Additionally, the public relations specialist needs to be a strong writer and speaker, with good interpersonal, leadership, and organizational skills.

EXPLORING

Almost any experience in working with other people will help you to develop strong interpersonal skills, which are crucial in public relations. The possibilities are almost endless. Summer work on a newspaper or trade paper or with a radio or television station may give insight into communications media. Working as a volunteer on a political campaign can help you to understand the ways in which people can be persuaded. A summer job in the public relations department of a major charity or nonprofit organization will help you understand the unique demands of this field. Being selected as a page for the U.S. Congress or a state legislature will help you grasp the fundamentals of government processes. A job in retail will help you to understand some of the principles of product presentation. A teaching job will develop your organization and presentation skills. These are just some of the jobs that will let you explore areas of public relations.

EMPLOYERS

Public relations specialists hold about 188,000 jobs. Workers may be paid employees of the organization they represent or they may be part of a public relations firm that works for organizations on a contract basis. Others are involved in fund-raising or political campaigning. Public relations may be done for a nonprofit organization, educational institution, association, corporation, retail business, service company, or utility.

Most PR firms are located in large cities that are centers of communications. New York, Chicago, San Francisco, Los Angeles, and Washington, D.C., are good places to start a search for a public relations job. Nevertheless, there are many good opportunities in cities across the United States.

STARTING OUT

There is no clear-cut formula for getting a job in public relations. Individuals often enter the field after gaining preliminary experience in another occupation closely allied to the field, usually some segment of communications, and frequently, in journalism. Coming into public relations from newspaper work is still a recommended route. Another good method is to gain initial employment as a public relations trainee or intern, or as a clerk, secretary, or research assistant in a public relations department or a counseling firm.

ADVANCEMENT

In some large companies, an entry-level public relations specialist may start as a trainee in a formal training program for new employees. In others, new employees may expect to be assigned to work that has a minimum of responsibility. They may assemble clippings or do rewrites on material that has already been accepted. They may make posters or assist in conducting polls or surveys, or compile reports from data submitted by others.

As workers acquire experience, they are typically given more responsibility. They write news releases, direct polls or surveys, or advance to writing speeches for company officials. Progress may seem to be slow, because some skills take a long time to master.

Some advance in responsibility and salary in the same firm or organization in which they started. Others find that the path to advancement is to accept a more rewarding position in another firm.

The goal of many public relations specialists is to open an independent office or to join an established consulting firm. To start an independent office requires a large outlay of capital and an established reputation in the field. However, those who are successful in operating their own consulting firms probably attain the greatest financial success in the public relations field.

EARNINGS

According to *Compensation in Nonprofit Organizations 2006*, a report from Abbott, Langer & Associates, directors of public relations had median annual incomes of $52,038 in 2006, while public relations assistants earned $40,000. Salaries for public relations specialists employed in all industries ranged from less than $28,080 to more than $89,220 in 2006, according to the U.S. Department of Labor.

Many PR workers receive a range of fringe benefits from corporations, agencies, and organizations employing them, including bonus/incentive compensation, stock options, profit sharing/pension plans/401(k) programs, medical benefits, life insurance, financial planning, maternity/paternity leave, paid vacations, and family college tuition.

Bonuses can range from 5 to 100 percent of base compensation and often are based on individual and/or company performance.

WORK ENVIRONMENT

Public relations specialists generally work in offices with adequate secretarial help, regular salary increases, and expense accounts. They are expected to make a good appearance in tasteful, conservative clothing. They must have social poise, and their conduct in their personal life is important to their firms or their clients. The public relations specialist may have to entertain business associates.

The PR specialist seldom works conventional office hours for many weeks at a time; although the workweek may consist of 35 to 40 hours, these hours may be supplemented by evenings and even weekends when meetings must be attended and other special events covered. Time behind the desk may represent only a small part of the total working schedule. Travel is often an important and necessary part of the job.

The life of the PR worker is so greatly determined by the job that many consider this a disadvantage. Because the work is concerned with public opinion, it is often difficult to measure the results of performance and to sell the worth of a public relations program to an employer or client. Competition in the consulting field is keen, and if a firm loses an account, some of its personnel may be affected. The demands it makes for anonymity will be considered by some as one of the profession's less inviting aspects. Public relations involves much more hard work and a great deal less glamour than is popularly supposed.

OUTLOOK

Employment of public relations professionals is expected to grow faster than the average for all occupations through 2014, according to the U.S. Department of Labor. Competition will be keen for beginning jobs in public relations because so many job seekers are enticed by the perceived glamour and appeal of the field; those with both education and experience will have an advantage.

Most large companies and organizations have some sort of public relations resource, either through their own staff or through the use of a firm of consultants. Most are expected to expand their public relations activities, creating many new jobs. More smaller companies and organizations are hiring public relations specialists, adding to the demand for these workers. Additionally, as a result of recent corporate scandals, more public relations specialists will be hired to help improve the images of companies and regain the trust of the public.

Opportunities for public relations specialists in the nonprofit industry should also be good. Approximately 1.4 million nonprofit organizations are registered with the Internal Revenue Service, and many employ PR specialists to help them educate people about their programs.

FOR MORE INFORMATION

For information on accreditation, contact
International Association of Business Communicators
One Hallidie Plaza, Suite 600
San Francisco, CA 94102-2818
Tel: 800-776-4222
http://www.iabc.com

For statistics, salary surveys, and information on accreditation and student membership, contact
Public Relations Society of America
33 Maiden Lane, 11th Floor
New York, NY 10038-5150
Tel: 212-460-1400
Email: prssa@prsa.org (student membership)
http://www.prsa.org

This professional association for public relations professionals offers an accreditation program and opportunities for professional development.
Canadian Public Relations Society Inc.
4195 Dundas Street West, Suite 346
Toronto, ON M8X 1Y4 Canada
Tel: 416-239-7034
Email: admin@cprs.ca
http://www.cprs.ca

Rehabilitation Counselors

OVERVIEW

Rehabilitation counselors provide counseling and guidance services to people with disabilities to help them resolve life problems and to train for and locate work that is suitable to their physical and mental abilities, interests, and aptitudes. There are approximately 131,000 rehabilitation counselors working in the United States.

HISTORY

Today it is generally accepted that people with disabilities can and should have the opportunity to become as fully independent as possible in all aspects of life, from school to work and social activities. In response to the needs of disabled war veterans, Congress passed the first Vocational Rehabilitation Act in 1920. The act set in place the Vocational Rehabilitation Program, a federal-state program that provides for the delivery of rehabilitation services, including counseling, to eligible people with disabilities.

The profession of rehabilitation counseling has its roots in the Rehabilitation Act, which allowed for funds to train personnel. What was at first a job title developed into a fully recognized profession as it became evident that the delivery of effective rehabilitation services required highly trained specialists. Early efforts for providing rehabilitation counseling and other services were often directed especially toward the nation's veterans. In 1930, the Veterans Administration was created to supply support services to veterans and their families, and in 1989, the U.S. Department of Veterans Affairs was created as the 14th cabinet department in the U.S. government.

The passage of the Americans with Disabilities Act in 1990 recognized the rights and needs of people with disabilities and developed federal regulations and guidelines aimed at eliminating discrimination and other barriers preventing people with disabilities from participating fully in school, workplace, and public life. Many state and federal programs have since been created to aid people with disabilities.

THE JOB

Rehabilitation counselors work with people with disabilities to identify barriers to medical, psychological, personal, social, and vocational functioning and to develop a plan of action to remove or reduce those barriers.

Clients are referred to rehabilitation programs from many sources. Sometimes they seek help on their own initiative; sometimes their families bring them in. They may be referred by a physician, hospital, or social worker, or they may be sent by employment agencies, schools, or accident commissions. A former employer may seek help for the individual.

The counselor's first step is to determine the nature and extent of the disability and evaluate how that disability interferes with work and other life functions. This determination is made from medical and psychological reports as well as from family history, educational background, work experience, and other evaluative information.

The next step is to determine a vocational direction and plan of services to overcome the handicaps to employment or independent living.

The rehabilitation counselor coordinates a comprehensive evaluation of a client's physical functioning abilities and vocational interests, aptitudes, and skills. This information is used to develop vocational or independent-living goals for the client and the services necessary to reach those goals. Services that the rehabilitation counselor may coordinate or provide include physical and mental restoration, academic or vocational training, vocational counseling, job analysis, job modification or reasonable accommodation, and job placement. Limited financial assistance in the form of maintenance or transportation assistance may also be provided.

The counselor's relationship with the client may be as brief as a week or as long as several years, depending on the nature of the problem and the needs of the client.

REQUIREMENTS

High School

To prepare for a career in rehabilitation counseling, take your high school's college prep curriculum. These classes should include several years of mathematics and science, such as biology and chemistry. To begin to gain an understanding of people and societies, take history, psychology, and sociology classes. English classes are important to take because you will need excellent communication skills for this work. Some of your professional responsibilities will include documenting your work and doing research to provide your clients with helpful information; to do these things you will undoubtedly be working with computers. Therefore, you should take computer science classes so that you are skilled in using them. In addition, you may want to consider taking speech and a foreign language, both of which will enhance your communication skills.

Postsecondary Training

Although some positions are available for people with a bachelor's degree in rehabilitation counseling, these positions are usually as aides and offer limited advancement opportunities. Most employers require the rehabilitation counselors working for them to hold master's degrees. Before receiving your master's, you will need to complete a bachelor's degree with a major in behavioral sciences, social sciences, or a related field. Another option is to complete an undergraduate degree in rehabilitation counseling. Keep in mind, however, that even if you get an undergraduate degree in rehabilitation, you will still need to attend a graduate program to qualify for most counselor positions. No matter which undergraduate program you decide on, you should concentrate on courses in sociology, psychology, physiology, history, and statistics as well as courses in English and communications. Several universities now offer courses in various aspects of physical therapy and special education training. Courses in sign language, speech therapy, and a foreign language are also beneficial.

Both the Council for Accreditation of Counseling and Related Educational Programs and the Council on Rehabilitation Education accredit graduate counseling programs. A typical master's program in rehabilitation counseling usually lasts two years. Studies include courses in medical aspects of disability, psychosocial aspects of disability, testing techniques, statistics, personality theory, personality development, abnormal psychology, techniques of counseling, occupational information, and vocational training and job placement. A supervised internship is also an important aspect of a program.

Certification or Licensing

The regulation of counselors is required in 48 states and the District of Columbia. This regulation may be in the form of credentialing, registry, certification, or licensure. Regulations, however, vary by state and sometimes by employer. For example, an employer may require certification even if the state does not. You will need to check with your state's licensing board as well as your employer for specific information about your circumstances.

Across the country, many employers now require their rehabilitation counselors to be certified by the Commission on Rehabilitation Counselor Certification (CRCC). The purpose of certification is to provide assurance that professionals engaged in rehabilitation counseling meet set standards and maintain those standards through continuing education. To become certified, counselors must pass an extensive written examination to demonstrate their knowledge of rehabilitation counseling. The CRCC requires the master's degree as the minimum educational level for certification. Applicants who meet these certification requirements receive the designation of certified rehabilitation counselor.

Most state government rehabilitation agencies require future counselors to meet state civil service and merit system regulations. The applicant must take a competitive written examination and may also be interviewed and evaluated by a special board.

Other Requirements

The most important personal attribute required for rehabilitation counseling is the ability to get along well with other people. Rehabilitation counselors work with many different kinds of clients and must be able to see situations and problems from their client's point of view. They must be both patient and persistent. Rehabilitation may be a slow process with many delays and setbacks. The counselor must maintain a calm, positive manner even when no progress is made.

EXPLORING

To explore a career in which you work with people with disabilities, you should look for opportunities to volunteer or work in this field. One possibility is to be a counselor at a children's camp for disabled youngsters. You can also volunteer with a local vocational rehabilitation agency or a facility such as the Easter Seal Society or Goodwill. Other possibilities include reading for the blind or leading a hobby or craft class at an adult day care center. And don't forget volunteer opportunities at a local hospital or nursing home. Even if your only responsibility is to escort people to the X-ray department or talk to patients to cheer them up, you will gain valuable experience interacting with people who are facing challenging situations.

EMPLOYERS

Approximately 131,000 rehabilitation counselors are employed in the United States. Counselors work in a variety of settings. About three-quarters of rehabilitation counselors work for state agencies, some also work for local and federal agencies. Employment opportunities are available in rehabilitation centers, mental health agencies, developmental disability agencies, sheltered workshops, training institutions, and special schools. Other rehabilitation counselors teach at colleges and universities.

STARTING OUT

School career services offices are the best places for the new graduate to begin the career search. In addition, the National Rehabilitation Counseling Association and the American Rehabilitation Counseling Association (a division of the American Counseling Association) are sources for employment information. The new counselor may also apply directly to agencies for available positions. State and local vocational rehabilitation agencies employ about 10,000 rehabilitation counselors. The Department of Veterans Affairs employs counselors to assist with the rehabilitation of disabled veterans. Many rehabilitation counselors are employed by private for-profit or nonprofit rehabilitation programs and facilities. Others are employed in industry, schools, hospitals, and other settings, while others are self-employed.

ADVANCEMENT

The rehabilitation counselor usually receives regular salary increases after gaining experience in the job. He or she may move from relatively easy cases to increasingly challenging ones. Counselors may advance into such positions as administrator or supervisor after several years of counseling experience. It is also possible to find related counseling and teaching positions, which may represent an advancement in other fields.

EARNINGS

Salaries for rehabilitation counselors vary widely according to state, community, employer, and the counselor's experience. The U.S. Department of Labor reports that median annual earnings of rehabilitation counselors in 2006 were $29,200. Salaries ranged from less than $19,260 to more than $53,170.

Rehabilitation counselors employed by the federal government generally start at the GS-9 or GS-11 level. In 2007, basic GS-9 salary was $38,224. Those with master's degrees generally began at the GS-11 level, with a salary of $46,974 in 2007. Salaries for federal government workers vary according to the region of the country in which they work. Those working in areas with a higher cost of living receive additional locality pay.

Counselors employed by government and private agencies and institutions generally receive health insurance, pension plans, and other benefits, including vacation, sick, and holiday pay. Self-employed counselors must provide their own benefits.

WORK ENVIRONMENT

Rehabilitation counselors work approximately 40 hours each week and do not usually have to work during evenings or weekends. They work both in the office and in the field. Depending on the type of training required, lab space and workout or therapy rooms may be available. Rehabilitation counselors must usually keep detailed accounts of their progress with clients and write reports. They may spend many hours traveling about the community to visit employed clients, prospective employers, trainees, or training programs.

OUTLOOK

The passage of the Americans with Disabilities Act of 1990 increased the demand for rehabilitation counselors. As more local, state, and federal programs are initiated that are designed to assist people with disabilities and as private institutions and companies seek to comply with this new legislation, job prospects are promising. Budget pressures may serve to limit the number of new rehabilitation counselors to be hired by government agencies; however, the overall outlook remains excellent.

The U.S. Department of Labor predicts that employment for all counselors will grow faster than the average for all occupations through 2014. Some of this growth can be attributed to the advances in medical technology that are saving more lives. In addition, more employers are offering employee assistance programs that provide mental health and alcohol and drug abuse services.

FOR MORE INFORMATION

For general information on careers in rehabilitation counseling, contact
American Rehabilitation Counseling Association
5999 Stevenson Avenue
Alexandria, VA 22304-3300
Tel: 800-347-6647
http://www.arcaweb.org

For information on certification, contact
Commission on Rehabilitation Counselor Certification
300 North Martingale Road, Suite 460
Schaumburg, IL 60173-2088
Tel: 847-944-1325
Email: info@crccertification.com
http://www.crccertification.com

*For listings of CORE-approved programs as well as other informa-
tion, contact*
Council on Rehabilitation Education (CORE)
300 North Martingale Road, Suite 460
Schaumburg, IL 60173-2088
Tel: 847-944-1345
http://www.core-rehab.org

To learn about government legislation, visit the NRA's Web site.
National Rehabilitation Association (NRA)
633 South Washington Street
Alexandria, VA 22314-4109
Tel: 703-836-0850
Email: info@nationalrehab.org
http://www.nationalrehab.org

*The NRCA is a division of the National Rehabilitation Associa-
tion. For news on legislation, employment, and other information,
contact*
National Rehabilitation Counseling Association (NRCA)
PO Box 4480
Manassas, VA 20108-4480
Tel: 703-361-2077
Email: NRCAOFFICE@aol.com
http://nrca-net.org

For information on a variety of resources, contact
National Clearinghouse of Rehabilitation Training Materials
Utah State University
6524 Old Main Hill
Logan, UT 84322-6524
Tel: 866-821-5355
Email: ncrtm@cc.usu.edu
http://ncrtm.org

Social Workers

QUICK FACTS

School Subjects
Health
Psychology

Personal Skills
Communication/ideas
Helping/teaching

Work Environment
Primarily indoors
Primarily multiple locations

Minimum Education Level
Bachelor's degree

Salary Range
$22,490 to $40,000 to
$64,070+

Certification or Licensing
Required

Outlook
Faster than the average

DOT
195

GOE
12.02.02

NOC
4152

O*NET-SOC
21-1021.00, 21-1022.00,
21-1023.00

OVERVIEW

Social workers help people and assist communities in solving problems. These problems include poverty, racism, discrimination, physical and mental illness, addiction, and abuse. They counsel individuals and families, they lead group sessions, they research social problems, and they develop policy and programs. Social workers are dedicated to empowering people and helping them to preserve their dignity and worth. Approximately 562,000 social workers are employed in the United States.

HISTORY

Even before the United States became a country, poverty and unemployment were among society's problems. Almshouses and shelters that provided the homeless with jobs and rooms were established as early as 1657. The social work profession as we know it today, however, has its origins in the "friendly visitor" of the early 1800s; these charity workers went from home to home offering guidance in how to move beyond the troubles of poverty.

At a time when not much financial assistance was available from local governments, the poor relied on friendly visitors for instruction on household budgeting and educating their children. Despite their good intentions, however, the friendly visitors could not provide the poor with all the necessary support. The middle-class women who served as friendly visitors were generally far removed from the experiences of the lower classes. Most of the friendly visitors served the community for only a very short time and therefore did not have the opportunity to gain much experience with the poor. The great difference between the life experiences of the friendly visitors and the experiences of their clients sometimes resulted in serious problems: The self-esteem and ambitions of the poor were damaged by the moral judgments of the friendly visitors. In some cases, friendly visitors served only to promote their middle-class values and practices. By the late 1800s, many charitable organizations developed in U.S. and Canadian cities. With the development of these organizations came a deeper insight into improving the conditions of the poor. Serving as a friendly visitor came to be considered an apprenticeship; it became necessary for friendly visitors to build better relationships with their clients. Friendly visitors were encouraged to take the time to learn about their clients and to develop an understanding of each client's individual needs. Nevertheless, some sense of moral superiority remained, as these charitable organizations refused assistance to alcoholics, beggars, and prostitutes.

The birth of the settlement house brought charity workers even closer to their clients. Settlement houses served as communities for the poor and were staffed by young, well-educated idealists anxious to solve society's problems. The staff people lived among their clients and learned from them. In 1889, Jane Addams established the best known of the settlement houses, a community in Chicago called Hull House. Addams wrote extensively about the problems of the poor, and her efforts to provide solutions to their problems led to the foundation of social work education. She emphasized the importance of an education specific to the concerns of the social worker. By the 1920s, social work master's degree programs were established in many universities.

Theories and methodologies of social work have changed over the years, but the basis of the profession has remained the same: helping people and addressing social problems. As society changes, so do its problems, calling for redefinition of the social work profession. The first three fields of formal social work were defined by setting: medical social work, psychiatric social work, and child welfare. Later, practice was classified by different methodologies: casework, group work, and community organization. Most recently, the social work profession has been divided into two areas—direct practice and indirect practice.

THE JOB

After months of physical abuse from her husband, a young woman has taken her children and moved out of her house. With no job and no home, and fearing for her safety, she looks for a temporary shelter for herself and her children. Once there, she can rely on the help of social workers who will provide her with a room, food, and security. The social workers will offer counseling and emotional support to help her address the problems in her life. They will involve her in group sessions with other victims of abuse. They will direct her to job training programs and other employment services. They will set up interviews with managers of low-income housing. As the woman makes efforts to improve her life, the shelter will provide day care for the children. All these resources exist because the social work profession has long been committed to empowering people and improving society.

The social worker's role extends even beyond the shelter. If the woman has trouble getting help from other agencies, the social worker will serve as an advocate, stepping in to ensure that she gets the aid to which she is entitled. The woman may also qualify for long-term assistance from the shelter, such as a second-step program in which a social worker offers counseling and other support over several months. The woman's individual experience will also help in the social worker's research of the problem of domestic violence; with that research, the social worker can help the community come to a better understanding of the problem and can direct society toward solutions. Some of these solutions may include the development of special police procedures for domestic disputes, or court-ordered therapy groups for abusive spouses.

Direct social work practice is also known as *clinical practice*. As the name suggests, direct practice involves working directly with the client by offering counseling, advocacy, information and referral, and education. *Indirect practice* concerns the structures through which the direct practice is offered. Indirect practice (a practice consisting mostly of social workers with Ph.D. degrees) involves program development and evaluation, administration, and policy analysis. The vast majority of the 150,000 members of the National Association of Social Workers (NASW) work in direct service roles.

Because of the number of problems facing individuals, families and communities, social workers find jobs in a wide variety of settings and with a variety of client groups. Some of these areas are discussed in the paragraphs that follow.

Health/mental health care. Mental health care has become the lead area of social work employment. These jobs are competitive and typically go to more experienced social workers. Settings include community mental health centers, where social workers serve persistently mentally ill people and participate in outreach services; state and county mental hospitals, for long-term, inpatient care; facilities of the Department of Veterans Affairs, involving a variety of mental health care programs for veterans; and private psychiatric hospitals, for patients who can pay directly.

Social workers also work with patients who have physical illnesses. They help individuals and their families adjust to the illness and the changes that illness may bring to their lives. They confer with physicians and with other members of the medical team to make plans about the best way to help the patient. They explain the treatment and its anticipated outcome to both the patient and the family. They help the patient adjust to the possible prospect of long hospitalization and isolation from the family.

Child care/family services. Efforts are being made to offer a more universal system of care that would incorporate child care, family services, and community service. Child care services include day care homes, child care centers, and Head Start centers. Social workers in this setting attempt to address all the problems children face from infancy to late adolescence. They work with families to detect problems early and intervene when necessary. They research the problems confronting children and families, and they establish new services or adapt existing services to address these problems. They provide parenting education to teenage parents, which can involve living with a teenage mother in a foster care situation, teaching parenting skills, and caring for the baby while the mother attends school. Social workers alert employers to employees' needs for daytime child care.

Social workers in this area of service are constantly required to address new issues. In recent years, for example, social workers have developed services for families composed of different cultural backgrounds, services for children with congenital disabilities resulting from the mother's drug use, and disabilities related to HIV or AIDS.

Geriatric social work. Within this field, social workers provide individual and family counseling services in order to assess the older person's needs and strengths. Social workers help older people locate transportation and housing services. They also offer adult day care services, or adult foster care services that match older people with families. Adult protective services protect older people from abuse and neglect, and respite services allow family members time off from the care of an older person. A little-recognized problem is the rising incidence of HIV/AIDS among the elderly; 25 percent of all HIV/AIDS patients are aged 50 or over.

School social work. In schools, social workers serve students and their families, teachers, administrators, and other school staff members. Education, counseling, and advocacy are important aspects of school social work. With education, social workers attempt to prevent alcohol and drug abuse, teen pregnancy, and the spread of HIV/AIDS and other sexually transmitted diseases. They provide multicultural and family life education. They counsel students who are discriminated against because of their sexual orientation or racial, ethnic, or religious background. They also serve as advocates for these students, bringing issues of discrimination before administrators, school boards, and student councils.

A smaller number of social workers are employed in the areas of *social work education* (a field composed of the professors and instructors who teach and train students of social work); *group practice* (in which social workers facilitate treatment and support groups); and *corrections* (providing services to inmates in penal institutions). Social workers also offer counseling, occupational assistance, and advocacy to those with addictions and disabilities, to the homeless, and to women, children, and the elderly who have been in abusive situations.

Client groups expand and change as societal problems change. Social work professionals must remain aware of the problems affecting individuals and communities in order to offer assistance to as many people as possible.

Computers have become important tools for social workers. Client records are maintained on computers, allowing for easier collection and analysis of data. Interactive computer programs are used to train social workers, as well as to analyze case histories (such as for an individual's risk of HIV infection).

REQUIREMENTS

High School

To prepare for a social work career, you should take courses in high school that will improve your communications skills, such as English, speech, and composition. On a debate team, you could further develop your skills in communication as well as research and analysis. History, social studies, and sociology courses are important in understanding the concerns and issues of society. Although some work is available for those with only a high school diploma or associate's degree (as a

A social worker discusses a resettlement plan with a young woman in a homeless hostel. *(John Birdsall, The Image Works)*

social work aide or social services technician), the most opportunities exist for people with degrees in social work.

Postsecondary Training
There are approximately 442 accredited BSW (bachelor's in social work) programs and 168 accredited MSW (master's in social work) programs accredited by the Council on Social Work Education. The Group for the Advancement of Doctoral Education lists 80 doctoral programs for Ph.D.'s in social work or DSW (doctor of social work). The Council on Social Work Education requires that five areas be covered in accredited bachelor's degree social work programs: human behavior and the social environment; social welfare policy and services; social work practice; research; and field practicum. Most programs require two years of liberal arts study followed by two years of study in the social work major. Also, students must complete a field practicum of at least 400 hours. Graduates of these programs can find work in public assistance or they can work with the elderly or with people with mental or developmental disabilities.

Although no clear lines of classification are drawn in the social work profession, most supervisory and administrative positions require at least an MSW degree. Master's programs are organized according to fields of practice (such as mental health care), problem areas (substance abuse), population groups (the elderly), and practice roles (practice with individuals, families, or communities). They are usually two-year programs that require at least 900 hours of field practice. Most positions in mental health care facilities require an MSW. Doctoral degrees are also available and prepare students for research and teaching. Most social workers with doctorates go to work in community organizations.

Certification or Licensing
Licensing, certification, or registration of social workers is required by all states. To receive the necessary licensing, a social worker will typically have to gain a certain amount of experience and also pass an exam. The certification programs help to identify those social workers who have gained the knowledge and experience necessary to meet national standards.

The National Association of Social Workers offers three voluntary credentials and seven specialty certifications (five for MSWs and two for BSWs). Contact the association for more information.

Other Requirements
Social work requires great dedication. As a social worker, you have the responsibility of helping whole families, groups, and communi-

ties, as well as focusing on the needs of individuals. Your efforts will not always be supported by society at large; sometimes you must work against a community's prejudice, disinterest, and denial. You must also remain sensitive to the problems of your clients, offering support, and not moral judgment or personal bias. The only way to effectively address new social problems and new client groups is to remain open to the thoughts and needs of all human beings. Assessing situations and solving problems requires clarity of vision and a genuine concern for the well-being of others.

With this clarity of vision, your work will be all the more rewarding. Social workers have the satisfaction of making a connection with other people and helping them through difficult times. Along with the rewards, however, the work can cause a great deal of stress. Hearing repeatedly about the deeply troubled lives of prison inmates, the mentally ill, abused women and children, and others can be depressing and defeating. Trying to convince society of the need for changes in laws and services can be a long, hard struggle. You must have perseverance to fight for your clients against all odds.

EXPLORING

As a high school student, you may find openings for summer or part-time work as a receptionist or file clerk with a local social service agency. If there are no opportunities for paid employment, you could work as a volunteer. You can also gain good experience by working as a counselor in a camp for children with physical, mental, or developmental disabilities. Your local YMCA, park district, or other recreational facility may need volunteers for group recreation programs, including programs designed for the prevention of delinquency. By reporting for your high school newspaper, you'll have the opportunity to interview people, conduct surveys, and research social change, all of which are important aspects of the social work profession.

You could also volunteer a few afternoons a week to read to people in retirement homes or to the blind. Work as a tutor in special education programs is sometimes available to high school students.

EMPLOYERS

Approximately 562,000 social workers are employed in the United States. Social workers can be employed in direct or clinical practice, providing individual and family counseling services, or they may work as administrators for the organizations that provide direct practice. Social workers are employed by community health and mental health centers; hospitals and mental hospitals; child care, family services, and community service organizations, including day care and Head Start programs; elderly care programs, including adult protective services and adult day care and foster care; prisons; shelters and half-way houses; schools; courts; and nursing homes.

STARTING OUT

Most students of social work pursue a master's degree and in the process learn about the variety of jobs available. They also make valuable connections through faculty and other students. Through the university's career services office or an internship program, a student will learn about job openings and potential employers.

A social work education in an accredited program will provide you with the most opportunities, and the best salaries and chances for promotion, but practical social work experience can also earn you full-time employment. A part-time job or volunteer work will introduce you to social work professionals who can provide you with career guidance and letters of reference. Agencies with limited funding may not be able to afford to hire social workers with MSWs and will therefore look for applicants with a great deal of experience and lower salary expectations.

ADVANCEMENT

More attractive and better-paying jobs tend to go to those with more years of practical experience. Dedication to your job, an extensive resume, and good references will lead to advancement in the profession. Also, many social work programs offer continuing education workshops, courses, and seminars. These refresher courses help practicing social workers to refine their skills and to learn about new areas of practice and new methods and problems. The courses are intended to supplement your social work education, not substitute for a bachelor's or master's degree. These continuing education courses can lead to job promotions and salary increases.

EARNINGS

The more education a social worker has completed, the more money he or she stands to make in the profession. The area of practice also determines earnings. The areas of mental health, group services, and community organization and planning provide higher salaries, while elderly and disabled care generally provide lower pay. Salaries also vary among regions. Social workers on the East and West Coasts earn higher salaries than those in the Midwest. During their first five years of practice, social workers' salaries generally increase faster than in later years.

The median salary for child, family, and school social workers was $37,480 in 2006, according to the U.S. Department of Labor. The top paid 10 percent earned more than $62,530, while the lowest paid 10 percent earned less than $24,480. Medical and public health social workers' salaries ranged from less than $27,280 to more than $64,070 with a median salary of $43,040 in 2006; mental health and substance abuse workers earned between $22,490 and $57,630 with a median salary of $35,410.

Most full-time positions provide life and medical insurance, pension plans, and paid vacation and holidays.

WORK ENVIRONMENT

Social workers do not always work at a desk. When they do, they may be interviewing clients, writing reports, or conferring with other staff members. Depending on the size of the agency, office duties such as typing letters, filing, and answering phones may be performed by an aide or volunteer. Social workers employed at shelters or halfway houses may spend most of their time with clients, tutoring, counseling, or leading groups.

Some social workers have to drive to remote areas to make a home visit. They may go into inner-city neighborhoods, schools, courts, or jails. In larger cities, domestic violence and homeless shelters are sometimes located in rundown or dangerous areas. Most social workers are involved directly with the people they serve and must carefully examine the client's living conditions and family relations. Although some of these living conditions can be pleasant and demonstrate a good home situation, others can be squalid and depressing.

Advocacy involves work in a variety of different environments. Although much of this work may require making phone calls and sending faxes, e-mails, and letters, it also requires meetings with clients' employers, directors of agencies, local legislators, and others. It may sometimes require testifying in court as well.

OUTLOOK

The field of social work is expected to grow faster than the average for all occupations through 2014, according to the U.S. Department of Labor. The greatest factor for this growth is the increased number of older people who are in need of social services. Social workers who specialize in gerontology will find many job opportunities in nursing homes, hospitals, and home health care agencies. The needs of the future elderly population are likely to be different from those of the present elderly. Currently, the elderly appreciate community living, while subsequent generations may demand more individual care.

Schools will also need more social workers to deal with issues such as teenage pregnancies, children from single-parent households, and any adjustment problems recent immigrants may have. The trend to integrate students with disabilities into the general school population will require the expertise of social workers to make the transition smoother. However, job availability in schools will depend on funding given by state and local sources.

To help control costs, hospitals are encouraging early discharge for some of their patients. Social workers will be needed by hospitals to help secure health services for patients in their homes. There is also a growing number of people with physical disabilities or impairments staying in their own homes, requiring home health care workers.

Increased availability of health insurance funding and the growing number of people able to pay for professional help will create opportunities for those in private practice. Many businesses hire social workers to help in employee assistance programs, often on a contractual basis.

Poverty is still a main issue that social workers address. Families are finding it increasingly challenging to make ends meet on wages that are just barely above the minimum. The problem of fathers who do not make their court-ordered child support payments forces single mothers to work more than one job or rely on welfare. An increased awareness of domestic violence has also focused attention on the fact that many homeless and unemployed people are women who have left abusive situations. Besides all this, working with the poor is often considered unattractive, leaving many social work positions in this area unfilled.

Competition for jobs in urban areas will remain strong. However, there is still a shortage of social workers in rural areas; these areas usually cannot offer the high salaries or modern facilities that attract large numbers of applicants.

The social work profession is constantly changing. The survival of social service agencies, both private and public, depends on shifting political, economic, and workplace issues.

Social work professionals are worried about the threat of declassification. Because of budget constraints and a need for more workers, some agencies have lowered their job requirements. When unable to afford qualified professionals, they hire those with less education and experience. This downgrading raises questions about quality of care and professional standards. Just as in some situations low salaries push out the qualified social worker, so do high salaries. In the area of corrections, attractive salaries (up to $40,000 for someone with a two-year associate's degree) have resulted in more competition from other service workers.

Liability is another growing concern. If a social worker, for example, tries to prove that a child has been beaten or attempts to remove a child from his or her home, the worker can potentially be sued for libel. At the other extreme, a social worker can face criminal charges for failure to remove a child from an abusive home. More social workers are taking out malpractice insurance.

FOR MORE INFORMATION

For information on social work careers and educational programs, contact
Council on Social Work Education
1725 Duke Street, Suite 500
Alexandria, VA 22314-3457
Tel: 703-683-8080
Email: info@cswe.org
http://www.cswe.org

To access the online publication Choices: Careers in Social Work, *contact*
National Association of Social Workers
750 First Street, NE, Suite 700
Washington, DC 20002-4241
Tel: 202-408-8600
http://www.naswdc.org

For information on educational programs in Canada, contact
Canadian Association of Schools of Social Work
1398 Star Top Road
Ottawa, ON K1B 4V7 Canada
Tel: 613-792-1953
Email: cassw@cassw-acess.ca
http://www.cassw-acess.ca

For career information and job listings available in Canada, contact
Canadian Association of Social Workers
383 Parkdale Avenue, Suite 402
Ottawa, ON K1Y 4R4 Canada
Tel: 613-729-6668
Email: casw@casw-acts.ca
http://www.casw-acts.ca

Statisticians

OVERVIEW

Statisticians use mathematical theories to collect and interpret information. This information is used to help various agencies, industries, and researchers determine the best ways to produce results in their work. There are approximately 19,000 statisticians in the United States, employed in a wide variety of work fields, including government, industry, private organizations, and scientific research.

HISTORY

One of the first known uses of statistical technique was in England in the mid-1800s, when a disastrous epidemic of cholera broke out in a section of London. A local physician named John Snow decided to conduct a survey to determine what sections of the city were affected by the disease. He then constructed a map showing how the infection was distributed and interviewed people who had survived the illness about their living habits. He discovered that everyone who had contracted the illness had drawn water from a certain pump in the area. Once the pump was sealed, the cholera epidemic subsided. Because of Snow's research, medical professionals were able to learn that cholera was transmitted through an infected water supply. His use of statistical methods therefore uncovered a fact that has since saved countless lives.

In its simplest form, statistics is a science that organizes many facts into a systematized picture of data. Modern statistics is based on the theory of probability, and the work of statisticians has been greatly enhanced by the invention of computers.

The need for statisticians has grown by leaps and bounds in modern times. Since 1945, the number of universities with programs leading

QUICK FACTS

School Subjects
Computer science
Mathematics

Personal Skills
Communication/ideas
Technical/scientific

Work Environment
Primarily indoors
Primarily one location

Minimum Education Level
Bachelor's degree

Salary Range
$37,010 to $57,500 to $122,750

Certification or Licensing
None available

Outlook
More slowly than the average

DOT
020

GOE
02.06.02

NOC
2161

O*NET-SOC
15-2041.00

to graduate degrees in statistics has jumped from a half-dozen to more than 200. One reason for the increased demand is that statistical methods have many important uses. Statistics are now used in all areas of science as well as in industry, business, and the nonprofit sector. Government officials are especially dependent on statistics—from politicians to education and social services officials to traffic controllers.

THE JOB

Statisticians use their knowledge of mathematics and statistical theory to collect and interpret information. They determine whether data are reliable and useful and search for facts that will help solve scientific and other types of questions.

Most statisticians work in one of three kinds of jobs: they may teach and do research at a large university, they may work in a government agency (such as the U.S. Census Bureau or the U.S. Department of Health and Human Services), or they may work in a business or industry. A few statisticians work in private consulting agencies and sell their services to industrial or government organizations. Other statisticians work in well-known public opinion research organizations. Their studies help us understand what groups of people think about major issues of the day or products on the market. Some statisticians work as researchers for nonprofit organizations. They might gather information to help support their organization's request for a grant, to further the organization's agenda (such as fighting global warming or increasing literacy among low-income students in a major city), or simply as a resource for the organization's members or employees.

There are two major areas of statistics: mathematical statistics and applied statistics. *Mathematical statisticians* are primarily theoreticians. They develop and test new statistical methods and theories and devise new ways in which these methods can be applied. They also work on improving existing methods and formulas.

Applied statisticians use existing theories or known formulas to make new predictions or discoveries. They may forecast population growth or economic conditions, estimate the spread of an infectious disease, predict and evaluate the result of a marketing program, or help engineers and scientists determine the best design for a jet airline.

In some cases, statisticians actually go out and gather the data to be analyzed. Usually, however, they receive data from individuals trained especially in research-gathering techniques. In the U.S. Census Bureau, for example, statisticians work with material that has been compiled by thousands of census takers. Once the census takers have gathered the data, they turn the information over to statisticians for organization, analysis, and conclusions or recommendations.

Statisticians are employed in many sectors of society. One of the largest employers of statisticians is the government, because many government operations depend on detailed estimates of activities. Government data on consumer prices, population trends, and employment patterns, for example, can affect public policy and social programs.

REQUIREMENTS

High School

If you are interested in the field of statistics, you should take classes that will prepare you for college, since you will need at least a bachelor's degree to qualify for jobs. Focus on mathematics, computers, and science classes, but don't neglect other college preparatory courses such as English and a foreign language.

Postsecondary Training

Statisticians usually graduate from college with strong mathematics and computer backgrounds. Bachelor's degrees in statistics, mathematics, or biostatistics are available at approximately 230 colleges and universities in the United States. Classes include differential and integral calculus, mathematical modeling, statistical methods, and probability. Other students major in the field they hope to work in, such as chemistry, agriculture, or psychology.

Although a bachelor's degree is the minimum needed to become a statistician, your chances for success are better if you earn an advanced degree. Many positions are open only to those with a master's or doctorate. Approximately 140 universities offer a master's degree program in statistics, and about 90 have doctorate programs in statistics.

Other Requirements

Prospective statisticians should be able to think in terms of mathematical concepts. More importantly, they should be able to think logically in order to effectively process statistics. Statisticians should also have a strong curiosity that will prompt them to explore any given subject. Finally, a good statistician should be detail oriented and able to handle stress well.

EXPLORING

While in high school, ask your math teachers to give you some simple statistical problems, perhaps related to grades or student government. This will allow you to practice the kinds of techniques that statisticians use. If you want to explore the profession further, you might visit a large nonprofit organization that employs statisticians, a local insurance agency, the local office of the Internal Revenue Service, or a nearby college and talk to people who use statistical methods.

College students can frequently obtain jobs as student assistants in the offices of faculty members who are engaged in some kind of research. Although these jobs may seem to carry little responsibility, undergraduate students can gain some insight into and practice in research methods.

EMPLOYERS

There are approximately 19,000 statisticians employed in the United States. About 20 percent of these workers are employed by the federal government, such as the Departments of Commerce, Health and Human Services, and Agriculture, as well as the Census Bureau. Another 20 percent work for state and local governments. Of the remaining statisticians, most work in private industry. Private-industry employers include nonprofit organizations, insurance companies, research and testing services, management and public relations firms, computer and data processing firms, manufacturing companies, and the financial services sector. Statisticians also work in colleges and universities in teaching and research positions.

Jobs for statisticians can be found throughout the United States but are concentrated most heavily in large metropolitan areas such as New York, Chicago, Los Angeles, and Washington, D.C.

STARTING OUT

Most new graduates find positions through their college career services offices. For those students who are particularly interested in working for a government agency, jobs are listed with the Office of Personnel Management. Some government jobs may be obtained only after the successful passing of a civil service examination. College-level teaching is normally only open to candidates with doctorates. College teaching jobs are usually obtained by making a direct application to the dean of the school or college in which the statistics department is located.

ADVANCEMENT

A statistician with a bachelor's degree will probably begin in a position that involves primarily routine or clerical work, such as the job of junior statistician. Advancement may be seen more in terms of gradually increased pay rather than greater job responsibilities. After having acquired experience on the job and value to the employer, the statistician may be promoted to chief statistician, director of research, or, in teaching positions, full professor. Advancement can take many years, and it usually requires returning to graduate school or a special technical school to achieve a higher degree or more skills. Statisticians who advance most rapidly to positions of responsibility are usually those with advanced degrees.

EARNINGS

The U.S Department of Labor reports that the median annual salary for statisticians employed in all industries was $65,720 in 2006; the highest paid group earned more than $108,630, while the lowest paid group earned less than $37,010. According to *Compensation in Nonprofit Organizations 2006*, a report from Abbott, Langer & Associates, chief statisticians had median annual incomes of $57,500 in 2006.

The income for statisticians working in colleges and universities differs, depending on their position and their amount of experience. According to the 2006-2007 Salary Report of Academic Statisticians from the American Statistical Association, the median salary for assistant professors working in research institutions ranged from $67,500 to $70,400 based on their amount of experience. Full professors might expect to earn anywhere from $93,550 to $122,750. In liberal arts institutions, assistant professors earned a median salary of $59,950. Full professors earned between $81,592 and $106,850 a year based on their amount of experience. Most statisticians receive a benefits package from their employer that typically includes paid sick and vacation time, health insurance, and some sort of retirement plan.

WORK ENVIRONMENT

Most statisticians work under pleasant circumstances, with regular work hours. In private industry or government, statisticians work in an office setting. Some may travel to collaborate on larger research projects. In academia, statisticians often split their time between teaching and conducting research. Because this field of work is so heavily computerized, most statisticians' jobs will include a substantial amount of time on a computer.

OUTLOOK

Employment for statisticians is expected to grow more slowly than the average for all occupations through 2014, according to the U.S. Department of Labor. Even so, trained statisticians with advanced degrees or specialized training in computer science, engineering, or finance will have good job opportunities.

Opportunities for statisticians employed in the nonprofit sector should only be fair in the next several years. Some nonprofit organizations are unable to hire statisticians due to budgetary constraints or because they do not have a steady need for their services.

The federal government will continue to need statisticians for various agencies (for example, in Social Security, environmental protection, and demography), though competition is predicted to be high. Private industry will continue to need statisticians, especially in the pharmaceutical and automobile industries.

Opportunities for statisticians increase with level of education. Graduates with a bachelor's degree in mathematics and computer science are most likely to find jobs in applied statistics in private industry or government. With proper licensing, they may teach statistics in high schools. In other cases, job seekers with bachelor's degrees may take entry-level jobs that do not have the formal job title of statistician. However, their work will involve much of the same processes, such as analyzing and interpreting data in economics, engineering, or biological science.

Statisticians with a master's degree and knowledge of computer science should find openings in private industry in statistical computing and in research. These candidates can also teach in junior colleges and small four-year colleges. The employment outlook is best for those with doctorates in statistics. These individuals are eagerly sought by large corporations as consultants, and they are also in demand by colleges and universities.

FOR MORE INFORMATION

For information on careers in statistics or schools that offer degrees in statistics, contact
American Statistical Association
732 North Washington Street
Alexandria, VA 22314-1943
Tel: 888-231-3473
Email: asainfo@amstat.org
http://www.amstat.org

For information on educational and employment opportunities in statistics and related fields, contact
Association for Women in Mathematics
11240 Waples Mill Road, Suite 200
Fairfax, VA 22030-6078

Tel: 703-934-0163
Email: awm@awm-math.org
http://www.awm-math.org

For information on nonprofit organizations, contact the following organizations:
Council on Foundations
1828 L Street, NW, Suite 300
Washington, DC 20036-5104
Tel: 202-466-6512
Email: info@cof.org
http://www.cof.org

Foundation Center
79 Fifth Avenue & 16th Street
New York, NY 10003-3076
Tel: 800-424-9836
http://foundationcenter.org

National Council of Nonprofit Associations
1101 Vermont Avenue, NW, Suite 1002
Washington, DC 20005-3560
Tel: 202-962-0322
http://www.ncna.org

For a brochure on careers in applied mathematics, contact or visit the following Web site:
Society for Industrial and Applied Mathematics
3600 Market Street, 6th Floor
Philadelphia, PA 19104-2688
Tel: 215-382-9800
http://www.siam.org

For information on schools and career opportunities in statistics in Canada, contact
Statistical Society of Canada
577 King Edward Avenue
Ottawa, ON K1N 6N5 Canada
Tel: 613-562-5320
Email: info@ssc.ca
http://www.ssc.ca

Tutors and Trainers

QUICK FACTS

School Subjects
Psychology
Speech

Personal Skills
Communication/ideas
Helping/teaching

Work Environment
Primarily indoors
Primarily multiple locations

Minimum Education Level
Bachelor's degree

Salary Range
$12,000 to $20,000 to
$26,400+

Certification or Licensing
Voluntary

Outlook
About as fast as the average

DOT
099 (tutors)
166 (trainers)

GOE
N/A (tutors)
13.02.01 (trainers)

NOC
N/A (tutors)
4131 (trainers)

O*NET-SOC
N/A (tutors)
13-1073.00 (trainers)

OVERVIEW

Tutors help people reach their full potential in many areas of study including reading, mathematics, and science. *Mentors* go beyond educational help and serve as advisors and role models for young people from disadvantaged backgrounds or others who may be new to a career or field of study. *Trainers* educate, train, and supervise tutors and mentors, and other volunteers according to the mission of the organization of which they belong.

HISTORY

Tutors have helped people master academic subjects and learn life skills for thousands of years. They have helped those who would be kings, the children of politicians and noblemen, and more recently, the disadvantaged, attain knowledge and live better lives through education.

In the nonprofit sector, tutors provide educational services to disadvantaged people. Tutoring is one of the most popular activities for volunteers, coming in second only to fund-raising, according to the U.S. Department of Labor. Tutors have many different educational, vocational, and societal backgrounds. What they do have in common is a sense of obligation to help those challenged by their lack of education or financial or social status. Trainers educate tutors regarding proper teaching methods, as well as teach other volunteers about their organization's mission, goals, and services.

Many tutors and trainers belong to the National Tutoring Association (NTA) an organization representing more than 5,000 tutors and trainers through the United States.

THE JOB

Tutors work in various capacities. Many elementary schools, high schools, and for-profit schools employ tutors to help in the instruction of their students. Tutors encourage the understanding of standard school subjects such as reading and math, assist with questions regarding homework, and work to improve a student's level of literacy. More importantly, tutors help students develop good learning habits. Many tutors associated with schools are paid employees; most have college degrees applicable to the subjects they tutor, for example a degree in education, mathematics, or English.

Tutors may also find positions with community organizations, such as the YMCA, which has locations throughout the United States, or local special interest groups such as the Asian Youth Center in San Gabriel, California. Since many of these operations are nonprofit, tutors are paid a small hourly wage, or, more often, volunteer.

Colleges and universities also hire tutors to help students. The Office of Academic Services at the University of Notre Dame, for example, hires tutors to work with its student athletes. Tutors are assigned to help student athletes gain a better understanding of their courses, and in the end become more organized and independent learners. Academic success is important for all students, but more so with student athletes, since grades determine their athletic eligibility.

Mentors are specialized tutors who help with academic challenges, but also provide guidance for college and career preparation, tips on improving social skills, and any other advice the individual may need. They act as role models for students. Their educational backgrounds vary, but most are successful professionals hoping to make a difference in a child's life. Mentoring activities include taking disadvantaged children to sporting and cultural events and museums, attending school functions, and essentially providing support in all aspects of the student's life.

Trainers work for educational centers, schools, and advocacy groups. They provide orientation, instruction, and scheduling for tutors, mentors, and other volunteers. Trainers prepare prospective tutors by teaching the basic concepts of tutoring, such as setting goals, lesson planning, communication skills, and positive reinforcement. They may also suggest different techniques based on the personality or age level of the student. For example, they may recommend that the tutor incorporate study with playtime for young children, and the use of multimedia technology with adults.

REQUIREMENTS

High School

In high school, take a well-rounded college preparatory curriculum. If you know the field that you'd like to tutor in, take as many classes as you can in that subject. For example, if you already know that you want to eventually tutor in math, you should take algebra, geometry, calculus, and any other math classes that are available. Taking speech and English courses will also help you hone your communication skills, which will be very important when you work with students.

Postsecondary Training

Tutors and trainers have a variety of educational backgrounds. Most tutors have a bachelor's degree or higher—usually in a field that is related to the area in which they tutor.

Certification or Licensing

The National Tutoring Association offers several voluntary certifications to tutors and related professionals. Contact the association for more information.

Other Requirements

Besides being skilled in the topics they teach, the best tutors are excellent communicators and are poised, friendly, and instantly at ease around new people. Tutors must also have great patience, especially if their student is having difficulty with a subject. Well-trained tutors will find other methods or approaches for teaching the lesson until the student understands the topic. Tutors should also be creative, oftentimes calling upon new inventive ways of instructing and inspiring their students.

Trainers should have strong communication skills, be organized, and enjoy teaching others.

EXPLORING

One way to begin exploring this field now is to talk to someone who is a tutor or trainer. Ask the following questions: What are your primary and secondary job duties? What are your typical work hours? What do you like most and least about your job? How did you train for this field? What advice would you give to young people who are interested in this career? You should also get involved in speech or drama clubs. Any experiences that you can get doing presentations or performing in front of a group will help you prepare for the field. Finally, volunteer to work as a tutor at your school or for a local community organization. This will give you a chance to learn about the career while helping someone improve his or her academic skills.

A tutor (left) helps a high school student with her homework. *(Jim West, The Image Works)*

EMPLOYERS

Tutors and trainers are employed by nonprofit organizations, corporations, and schools of all sizes. Although positions are available throughout the United States, the best opportunities can be found in large cities such as Chicago, New York, Washington, D.C., and Los Angeles.

STARTING OUT

Many nonprofit organizations and corporations offer opportunities to tutor or train; most positions are voluntary or provide a small stipend. You can research possible tutor positions on the Internet or ask a local charity or advocacy group if they need volunteers.

ADVANCEMENT

Tutors often advance by working with larger groups of students. However, they are most rewarded by having a student reach a hard-earned goal—becoming an accomplished reader, graduating from high school, or learning how to be a responsible adult. Some tutors with a passion for this line of work can become trainers for an organization or nonprofit group.

Trainers can advance by being assigned more tutors and mentors to train, by being promoted to higher-level positions within their organization, or by moving on to work at larger and more prestigious organizations.

EARNINGS

The U.S. Department of Labor does not provide salary information for tutors and trainers. According to industry estimates, salaried tutors may have earnings that range from $12,000 to $20,000 a year. According to *Compensation in Nonprofit Organizations 2006*, a report from Abbott, Langer & Associates, trainers had median annual incomes of $26,400 in 2006. Full-time tutors and trainers may receive benefits such as paid vacation days, sick leave, and health insurance.

WORK ENVIRONMENT

Tutors often need to travel in order to meet their students—especially if the student is a child without the means for transportation. They often meet at a mutually designated location—such as a classroom, library, bookstore, or at a tutoring center. Meeting places should be comfortable for both the student and tutor, and provide a quiet environment in which to learn. Some tutors may take their students on field trips to museums, zoos, workplaces, or cultural events to enhance a lesson.

Trainers typically work in comfortable office settings, but may travel offsite to monitor the work of tutors and mentors.

OUTLOOK

Tutors and trainers will always be in demand by nonprofit organizations, but aspiring tutors and trainers should know that these jobs—except positions with major foundations and nonprofit organizations—are often part time and low paying. Most tutors and trainers enter the field not for monetary gain, but because they want to help improve the lives of others. Job opportunities will be more readily available in large cities such as New York, Los Angeles, and Chicago that have many nonprofit organizations. Opportunities and pay will be better for tutors and trainers employed by for-profit organizations and companies.

FOR MORE INFORMATION

For information on tutoring, contact
National Tutoring Association
PO Box 6840
Lakeland, FL 33807-6840
Tel: 863-529-5206
Email: ntatutor@aol.com
http://www.ntatutor.org

Index

Entries and page numbers in **bold** indicate major treatment of a topic.

University of Notre Dame 179
University of Puerto Rico 83
urban communities. *See* cities

V

veterans, services for 14–15, 153
vocational counselors. *See* career and
  employment counselors
Vocational Rehabilitation Act 117, 153
vocational-rehabilitation counselors 16
Volunteer in Service to America
  (VISTA) 111, 114
volunteers 25–26, 27, 74, 110, 178
volunteers directors 24–31
voters, lobbying of 100

W

Wagner-Peyser Act 15
Wall Street Journal 95
Washington, D.C. 98
Welfare Reform Bill 107
Worldwide Initiatives for Grantmaker
  Support (WINGS) 45–46
Wundt, Wilhelm 125–126

Y

YMCA/YWCA 74, 179